Herodotus

Xerxes Invades Greece

TRANSLATED BY AUBREY DE SÉLINCOURT
REVISED BY JOHN MARINCOLA

PENGUIN EPICS

PENGUIN BOOKS

Published by the Penguin Group
Penguin Books Ltd, 80 Strand, London WC2R 0RL, England
Penguin Group (USA) Inc., 375 Hudson Street, New York, New York 10014, USA
Penguin Group (Canada), 90 Eglinton Avenue East, Suite 700, Toronto, Ontario, Canada M4P 2Y3
(a division of Pearson Penguin Canada Inc.)
Penguin Ireland, 25 St Stephen's Green, Dublin 2, Ireland (a division of Penguin Books Ltd)
Penguin Group (Australia), 250 Camberwell Road, Camberwell, Victoria 3124, Australia
(a division of Pearson Australia Group Pty Ltd)
Penguin Books India Pvt Ltd, 11 Community Centre, Panchsheel Park, New Delhi – 110 017, India
Penguin Group (NZ), cnr Airborne and Rosedale Roads, Albany,
Auckland 1310, New Zealand (a division of Pearson New Zealand Ltd)
Penguin Books (South Africa) (Pty) Ltd, 24 Sturdee Avenue,
Rosebank, Johannesburg 2196, South Africa

Penguin Books Ltd, Registered Offices: 80 Strand, London WC2R 0RL, England

www.penguin.com

The Histories first published in Penguin Classics 1954
Revised editions published 1972, 1996, 2003
This extract published in Penguin Books 2006

1

Translation copyright 1954 by Aubrey de Sélincourt
Revisions copyright © John Marincola, 1972, 1996, 2003
All rights reserved

Taken from the Penguin Classics edition of The Histories, translated by
Aubrey de Sélincourt, revised by John Marincola

Typeset by Rowland Phototypesetting Ltd, Bury St Edmunds, Suffolk
Printed in England by Clays Ltd, St Ives plc

ISBN-13: 978-0-141-02630-5
ISBN-10: 0-141-02630-8

Note

The Histories is one of the masterpieces of classical litera-
ture. Herodotus, who was described by Cicero as 'the
Father of History', recounts the epic struggle of a small
and quarrelsome band of Greek city states as they unite to
repel the might of the Persian Empire. His kaleidoscopic
blend of fact and legend gives the most vivid and com-
pelling view of the world in the fifth century BC.

This extract from *The Histories* tells the bloody tale of
the invasion of Greece, by Xerxes, King of Persia, and
his armies.

Xerxes, in the process of assembling his armies, had every corner of the continent ransacked. For the four years following the conquest of Egypt the mustering of troops and the provision of stores and equipment continued, and towards the close of the fifth Xerxes, at the head of his enormous force, began his march.

The army was indeed far greater than any other of which we know. It dwarfed the army Darius commanded on his Scythian campaign, and the great host of Scythians who burst into Media on the heels of the Cimmerians and brought nearly all upper Asia under their control. (It was this inroad which Darius' invasion was designed to avenge.) It was incomparably larger than the armies which the stories tell us Agamemnon and Menelaus led to Troy, or than those of the Mysians and Teucrians who before the Trojan War crossed the Bosphorus into Europe, overwhelmed Thrace, and, coming down to the Adriatic coast, drove as far south as the river Peneus. All these armies together, with others like them, would not have equalled the army of Xerxes. Was there a nation in Asia that he did not take with him against Greece? Save for the great rivers, was there a stream his army drank from that was not drunk dry? Some nations provided ships, others formed infantry units; from some cavalry was requisitioned, from others horse-transports and crews; from others, again, triremes for floating bridges, or provisions and naval craft of various kinds.

In view of the previous disaster to the fleet off Mt Athos, preparations had been going on in that area for the past three years. A fleet of triremes lay at Elaeus in the Chersonese, and from this base men of the various nations of which the army was composed were sent over in shifts to Athos, where they were put to the work of cutting a canal under the lash. The natives of Athos also took part. Bubares the son of Megabazus and Artachaees the son of Artaeus were the Persian officers in charge.

Mt Athos is a high and famous mountain running out into the sea. People live on it, and where the high land ends on the landward side it forms a sort of isthmus with a neck about a mile and a half wide, all of which is level ground or low hillocks, across from the sea by Acanthus to the sea facing Torone. On this isthmus where Athos peters out stands the Greek town of Sane, and south of it, on Athos itself, are Dium, Olophyxus, Acrothoon, Thyssus, and Cleonae – the inhabitants of which Xerxes now proposed to turn into islanders.

I will now describe how the canal was cut. The ground was divided into sections for the men of the various nations, on a line taped across the isthmus from Sane. When the trench reached a certain depth, the labourers at the bottom carried on with the digging and passed the soil up to others above them, who stood on terraces and passed it on to another lot, still higher up, until it reached the men at the top, who carried it away and dumped it. All the nations except the Phoenicians had their work doubled by the sides falling in, as they naturally would, since they made the cutting the same width at the top as it was intended to be at the bottom. But the Phoenicians, in this as in Xerxes' other works, gave a signal example of their skill. They, in the section allotted to them, took out a trench double the width prescribed for the actual finished canal, and by digging at a slope, contracted it as they got further down, until at the bottom their section was the same width as the rest.

In a meadow near by the workmen had their meeting-place and market, and grain ready ground was brought over in great quantity from Asia.

Thinking it over I cannot but conclude that it was mere ostentation that made Xerxes have the canal dug – he wanted to show his power and to leave something to be remembered by. There would have been no difficulty at all in getting the ships hauled across the isthmus on land; yet he ordered the construction of a channel for the sea broad enough for two triremes to be rowed abreast. The same people who had to cut the canal also had orders to bridge the river Strymon. At the same time other work too was in progress: cables, some of papyrus, some of white flax, were being prepared for the bridges – a task which Xerxes entrusted to the Phoenicians and Egyptians; and provision dumps were being formed for the troops, lest either men or animals should go hungry on the march to Greece. For these dumps the most convenient sites were chosen after a careful survey, the provisions being brought from many different parts of Asia in merchantmen or transport vessels. The greatest quantity was collected at a place called the White Cape in Thrace; other dumps were at

Tyrodiza in Perinthian territory, Doriscus, Eion on the Strymon, and in Macedonia.

So the work went on, and meanwhile the great army – all the troops from the continent which were to take part in the expedition – had assembled according to orders at Critalla in Cappadocia, and from there began to move forward with Xerxes to Sardis. Which of the Persian provincial governors received the king's prize for the best-equipped contingent, I am not able to say; nor do I even know if the matter was ever decided.

After crossing the Halys the army passed through Phrygia to Celaenae. In this place the springs of the river Maeander rise – and another river, too, of equal size, called (as its proper name) the Cataract. This latter stream rises in the actual market-square of Celaenae and joins the Maeander. Here, too, the skin of Marsyas the Silenus is exhibited; according to the Phrygian legend Apollo flayed Marsyas and hung the skin up here in the market-place. Here at Celaenae a Lydian named Pythius, the son of Atys, was awaiting Xerxes, and on his arrival entertained him and the whole army with most lavish hospitality, and promised besides to furnish money for the expenses of the war. The mention of money caused Xerxes to ask the Persians present who Pythius was and if he was really rich enough to make such an offer. 'My lord,' was the answer, 'it was this man who gave your father Darius the golden plane-tree and the golden vine; and still, so far as we know, he is the wealthiest man in the world, after yourself.'

Xerxes was amazed by this latter statement, and repeated his question, this time asking Pythius himself how much money he possessed. 'Sire,' said Pythius, 'I will be open with you and not pretend that I do not know the amount of my fortune. I do know it, and I will tell you exactly what it is. When I learned that you were on your way to the Aegean coast, my immediate wish was to make a contribution towards the expenses of the war; so I went into the matter of my finances and found upon calculation that I possessed 2000 talents of silver, and 3,993,000 gold Darics. This it is my intention to give you; I can live quite comfortably myself on my slaves and the produce of my estates.'

Xerxes was much pleased. 'My Lydian friend,' he replied, 'you are the only man I have met since I left Persian territory who has been willing to entertain my army, and nobody but you has come into my presence with an offer to contribute money for the war of his own free will. But you have done both, and on a magnificent scale. Therefore, as a reward for your generosity, I make you my guest-friend and, in addition, I will give you from my own coffers 7000 gold Darics which are needed to make your fortune up to the round sum of 4,000,000. Continue, then, to possess what you have acquired; and have the wisdom to remain always the man you have proved yourself today. You will never regret it, now or hereafter.'

Having carried out this promise, Xerxes moved on. Passing the Phrygian town of Anaua, and a lake from which salt is extracted, Xerxes now arrived at the large city of Colossae, where the river Lycus disappears underground to reappear about half a mile further on, where it, too, joins the Maeander. Leaving Colossae the army made for the Lydian border and arrived next at Cydrara, where a column with an inscription upon it set up by Croesus defines the boundary between Phrygia and Lydia. The road as it enters Lydia divides, one track leading left towards Caria, the other to the right towards Sardis. A traveller by the latter road has to cross the Maeander and pass Callatebus, a town where the manu-facture of honey out of tamarisk-syrup and wheat flour is carried on. This was the road which Xerxes took, and it was hereabouts that he came across a plane-tree of such beauty that he was moved to decorate it with golden ornaments and to appoint a guardian for it in perpetuity. The following day he reached the Lydian capital.

In Sardis Xerxes' first act was to send representatives to every place in Greece except Athens and Sparta with a demand for earth and water and a further order to prepare entertainment for him against his coming. This renewed demand for submission was due to his confident belief that the Greeks who had previously refused to comply with the demand of Darius would now be fright-ened into complying with his own. It was to prove whether or not he was right that he took this step.

He then prepared to move forward to Abydos, where a bridge had already been constructed across the Helles-pont from Asia to Europe. Between Sestos and Madytus in the Chersonese there is a rocky headland running out into the water opposite Abydos. It was here not long afterwards that the Athenians under Xanthippus the son of Ariphron took Artaÿctes the Persian governor of Sestos, and nailed him alive to a plank – he was the man who collected women in the temple of Protesilaus at Elaeus and committed various acts of sacrilege. This headland was the point to which Xerxes' engineers carried their two bridges from Abydos – a distance of seven furlongs. One was constructed by the Phoenicians using flax cables, the other by the Egyptians with papyrus cables. The work was successfully completed, but a subsequent storm of great violence smashed it up and carried everything away. Xerxes was very angry when he learned of the disaster, and gave orders that the Hellespont should receive three hundred lashes and have a pair of fetters thrown into it. I have heard before now that he also sent people to brand it with hot irons. He certainly instructed the men with the whips to utter, as they wielded them, the barbarous and presumptuous words: 'You salt and bitter stream, your master lays this punishment upon you for injuring him, who never injured you. But Xerxes the King will cross you, with or without your permission. No man sacrifices to you, and you deserve the neglect by your acid and muddy waters.' In addition to punishing the Hellespont Xerxes gave orders that the men responsible for building the bridges should have their heads cut off. The men who received these invidious orders duly carried them out, and other engineers completed the work. The method employed was as follows: penteconters and triremes were lashed together to support the bridges – 360 vessels for the one on the Black Sea side, and 314 for the other. They were moored slantwise to the Black Sea and at right angles to the Hellespont, in order to lessen the strain on the cables. Specially heavy anchors were laid out both upstream and downstream – those to the eastward to hold the vessels against winds blowing down the straits from the direction of the Black Sea, those on the other side, to the westward and towards the Aegean, to take the strain when it blew from the west and south. Gaps were left in three places to allow any boats that might wish to do so to pass in or out of the Black Sea.

Once the vessels were in position, the cables were hauled taut by wooden winches ashore. This time the two sorts of cable were not used separately for each bridge, but both bridges had two flax cables and four papyrus ones. The flax and papyrus cables were of the same thickness and quality, but the flax was the heavier – half a fathom of it weighed 114 lb. The next operation was to cut planks equal in length to the width of the floats, lay them edge to edge over the taut cables, and then bind them together on their upper surface. That done, brushwood was put on top and spread evenly, with a layer of soil, trodden hard, over all. Finally a paling was constructed along each side, high enough to prevent horses and mules from seeing over and taking fright at the water.

The bridges were now ready; and when news came from Athos that work on the canal was finished, including the breakwaters at its two ends, which had been built to prevent the surf from silting up the entrances, the army, after wintering at Sardis and completing its preparations, started the following spring on its march to Abydos.

No sooner had the troops begun to move than the sun vanished from his place in the sky and it grew dark as night, though the weather was perfectly clear and cloudless. Xerxes, deeply troubled, asked the Magi to interpret the significance of this strange phenomenon, and was given to understand that God meant to foretell to the Greeks the eclipse of their cities – for it was the sun which gave warning of the future to Greece, just as the moon did to Persia. Having heard this Xerxes continued the march in high spirits.

The army, however, had not gone far when Pythius the Lydian, in alarm at the sign from heaven, was emboldened by the presents he had received to come to Xerxes with a request. 'Master,' he said, 'there is a favour I should like you to grant me – a small thing, indeed, for you to perform, but to me of great importance, should you consent to do so.' Xerxes, who thought the request would be almost anything but what it actually turned out to be, agreed to grant it and told Pythius to say what it was he wanted. This generous answer raised Pythius' hopes, and he said, 'My lord, I have five sons, and it happens that every one of them is serving in your army in the campaign against Greece. I am an old man, Sire, and I beg you in pity to release from service one of my sons – the eldest – to take care of me and my property. Take the other four – and may you return with your purpose accomplished.'

Xerxes was furiously angry. 'You miserable fellow,' he cried, 'have you the face to mention your son, when I, in person, am marching to the war against Greece with my sons and brothers and kinsmen and friends – *you*, my slave, whose duty it was to come with me with every member of your house, including your wife? Mark my words: it is through the ears you can touch a man to pleasure or rage – let the spirit which dwells there hear good things, and it will fill the body with delight; let it hear bad, and it will swell with fury. When you did me good service, and offered more, you cannot boast that you were more generous than I; and now your punishment will be less than your impudence deserves. Yourself and four of your sons are saved by the entertainment you gave me; but you shall pay with the life of the fifth, whom you cling to most.'

Having answered Pythius in these words Xerxes at once gave orders that the men to whom such duties fell should find Pythius' eldest son and cut him in half and put the two halves one on each side of the road, for the army to march out between them. The order was performed.

And now between the halves of the young man's body the advance of the army began: first came the men with the gear and equipment, driving the pack-animals, and behind these a host of troops of all nationalities indiscriminately mixed. When more than half the army had passed, a gap was left in the marching column to keep these troops from contact with the king, who was immediately preceded by a thousand horsemen, picked out of all Persia, followed by a thousand similarly picked spearmen with spears reversed. Then came ten of the sacred horses, known as Nisaean, in magnificent harness. (The horses are so called because they come from the great Nisaean plain in Media, where horses of unusual size are bred.) They were followed by the holy chariot of Zeus drawn by eight white horses, with a charioteer on foot behind them holding the reins – for no mortal man may mount into that chariot's seat. Then came the king himself, riding in a chariot drawn by Nisaean horses, his charioteer, Patiramphes, son of Otanes the Persian, standing by his side.

That was how Xerxes rode from Sardis – and, when the fancy took him, he would leave his chariot and take his seat in a covered carriage instead. Behind him marched a thousand spearmen, their weapons pointing upwards in the usual way – all men of the best and noblest Persian blood; then a thousand picked Persian cavalry, then – again chosen for quality out of all that remained – a body of Persian infantry ten thousand strong. Of these a thousand had golden pomegranates instead of spikes on the butt-end of their spears, and were arrayed surrounding the other nine thousand, whose spears had silver pomegranates. The troops mentioned who marched with spears reversed also had golden pomegranates on the butt-end of their weapons, while those immediately behind Xerxes had golden apples. The ten thousand infantry were followed by a squadron of ten thousand Persian horse, after which there was a gap of two furlongs, and then came the remainder of the army, in a miscellaneous mass.

From Lydia the army made for the river Caicus and Mysia and thence proceeded through Atarneus to Carene, keeping Mt Cane on its left; then crossing the level country near Thebe it passed Atramyttium and the Pelasgian town of Antandrus, and with Mt Ida on its left entered Trojan territory. During a night in camp at the foot of Mt Ida a heavy storm of thunder and lightning caused the death of a considerable number of men. When the army reached the Scamander, the first river since the march from Sardis began which failed to provide enough water for men and beasts, Xerxes had a strong desire to see Troy, the ancient city of Priam. Accordingly he went up into the citadel, and when he had seen what he wanted to see and heard the story of the place from the people there, he sacrificed a thousand oxen to the Trojan Athene, and the Magi made libations of wine to the heroes. During the night which followed there was panic in the camp. At dawn the march continued; and the army after leaving on the left Rhoeteum, Ophryneum, and Dardanus which is next to Abydos, and the Teucrians of Gergithos on the right, arrived at Abydos.

[. . .]

All that day the preparations for the crossing continued; and on the following day, while they waited for the sun which they wished to see as it rose, they burned all sorts of spices on the bridges and laid boughs of myrtle along the way. Then sunrise came, and Xerxes poured wine into the sea out of a golden goblet and, with his face turned to the sun, prayed that no chance might prevent him from conquering Europe or turn him back before he reached its utmost limits. His prayer ended, he flung the cup into the Hellespont and with it a golden bowl and a Persian *acinaces*, or short sword. I cannot say for certain if he intended the things which he threw into the water to be an offering to the Sun-god; perhaps they were – or it may be that they were a gift to the Hellespont itself, to show he was sorry for having caused it to be lashed with whips.

This ceremony over, the crossing began. The infantry and cavalry went over by the upper bridge – the one nearer the Black Sea; the pack-animals and underlings by the lower one towards the Aegean. The first to cross were the Ten Thousand, all with wreaths on their heads, and these were followed by the mass of troops of all the nations. Their crossing occupied the whole of the first day. On the next day the first over were the thousand horsemen, and the contingent which marched with spears reversed – these, too, all wearing wreaths. Then came the sacred horses and the sacred chariot, and after them Xerxes himself with his spearmen and his thousand horsemen. The remainder of the army brought up the rear, and at the same time the ships moved over to the opposite shore. According to another account I have heard, the king crossed last.

From the European shore Xerxes watched his troops coming over under the whips. The crossing occupied seven days and nights without a break. There is a story that some time after Xerxes had passed the bridge, a native of the country thereabouts exclaimed: 'Why, O Zeus, have you assumed the shape of a man of Persia, and changed your name to Xerxes, in order to lead everyone in the world to the conquest and devastation of Greece? You could have destroyed Greece without going to that trouble.'

After the whole army had reached the European shore and the forward march had begun, a great portent occurred – a mare gave birth to a hare. Xerxes paid no attention to this omen, though the significance of it was easy enough to understand. Clearly it meant that he was to lead an army against Greece with the greatest pomp and circumstance, and then to come running for his life back to the place he started from. There had previously been another portent in Sardis, when a mule dropped a foal with a double set of sexual organs, male and female – the former uppermost. Xerxes, however, ignored both omens and continued his march at the head of the army. The fleet followed the coast in a westerly direction down the Hellespont and then on to Cape Sarpedon, where it had orders to wait, and thus started in the opposite direction to the army, which marched eastwards through the Chersonese, keeping on its right the tomb of Helle, the daughter of Athamas, and on its left the town of Cardia. After passing through a place called The Market, it skirted the Black Gulf and crossed the river which gives the gulf its name – and which failed on that occasion to supply enough water for the army's needs. From that point it turned west, past the Aeolian settlement of Aenus and Lake Stentoris, to Doriscus.

Doriscus is the name given to a strip of coast in Thrace backed by a large plain through which flows the large river Hebrus. A fortress – also called Doriscus – had been built here, and a Persian garrison left in it by Darius ever since his invasion of Scythia. It occurred to Xerxes, therefore, that it would be a convenient place for organizing and numbering his troops, and this he proceeded to do.

The naval captains had orders from Xerxes to move

all the ships from Doriscus to the adjoining beach where Zone stands, and the Samothracian town of Sale – the beach, that is, which runs out to the well-known headland of Serreum. In ancient times this whole district belonged to the Cicones. Here the ships were all hauled ashore and allowed to dry out.

Meanwhile Xerxes at Doriscus was occupied in numbering his troops. As nobody has left a record, I cannot state the precise number of men provided by each separate nation, but the grand total, excluding the naval contingent, turned out to be 1,700,000. The counting was done by first packing ten thousand men as close together as they could stand and drawing a circle round them on the ground; they were then dismissed, and a fence, about navel-high, was constructed round the circle; finally other troops were marched into the area thus enclosed and dismissed in their turn, until the whole army had been counted. After the counting, the army was reorganized in divisions according to nationality.

The nations of which the army was composed were as follows. First the Persians themselves: the dress of these troops consisted of the tiara, or soft felt cap, embroidered tunic with sleeves, a coat of mail looking like the scales of a fish, and trousers; for arms they carried large wicker shields, quivers slung below them, short spears, powerful bows with cane arrows, and daggers swinging from belts beside the right thigh. They were commanded by Otanes, the father of Xerxes' wife Amestris. In ancient times the Greek name for the Persians was Cephenes, though they were known to themselves and their neighbours as Artaei. It was not till Perseus, the son of Zeus and Danae, on a visit to Cepheus, the son of Belus, married his daughter Andromeda and had by her a son whom he named Perses (and left behind in that country because Cepheus had no male heir) that the Persians took, from this Perses, their present name.

The Median contingent, commanded by Tigranes the Achaemenid, was equipped in the same way as the Persian – in point of fact this mode of dress was originally Median and not Persian at all. The Medes were once universally known as Arians, but they, too, changed their name. In their case the change, according to their own account, followed the visit of Medea the Colchian, who went to their country from Athens.

The dress of the Cissian contingent was like the Persian, except that instead of caps they wore turbans. They were commanded by Anaphes, the son of Otanes. The Hyrcanians were armed in the same way as the Persians, and their commander was Megapanus, who afterwards became governor of Babylon. The Assyrians were equipped with bronze helmets made in a complicated barbarian way which is hard to describe: shields, spears, daggers (like the Egyptian ones), wooden clubs studded with iron, and linen corslets. These people used to be called Syrians by the Greeks, Assyrians being the name for them elsewhere. With them were the Chaldeans. Their commander was Otaspes, the son of Artachaees.

The Bactrians had caps almost exactly like those worn by the Medes, and were armed with their native cane bows and short spears. The Sacae (a Scythian people) wore trousers and tall pointed hats set upright on their heads, and were armed with the bows of their country, daggers, and the *sagaris*, or battle-axe. 'Sacae' is the name the Persians give to all Scythian tribes: these were the Amyrgian Scythians. They, together with the Bactrians, were under the command of Hystaspes, the son of Darius and of Cyrus' daughter Atossa.

The Indians were dressed in cotton; they carried cane bows and cane arrows tipped with iron, and marched under the command of Pharnazathres, the son of Artabates. The Arians, under Hydarnes' son Sisamnes, were armed with Median bows, the rest of their equipment being the same as the Bactrians'; also in Bactrian equipment were the Parthians and Chorasmians under Artabazus son of Pharnaces, the Sogdians under Azanes son of Artaeus, the Gandarians and Dadicae under Artyphius son of Artabanus. Then there were the Caspians and the Sarangians, the former commanded by Ariomardus, the brother of Artyphius, dressed in leather jackets and armed with the *acinaces* and the cane bow of their country; the latter, under Megabazus' son Pherendates, armed with bows and Median spears, and conspicuous for their brightly coloured clothes and high boots reaching to the knee. They were equipped with leather jackets, bows, and daggers. The Pactyan commander was Artaÿntes, the son of Ithamitres. The Utians and Myci under the command of Arsamenes son of Darius, and the Paricanians under Oeobazus' son Siromitres were equipped like the Pactyans.

The Arabians wore the *zeira*, caught in with a belt; their weapon was the bow, carried at the right side – a long bow, which assumed a reverse curve when unstrung. The Ethiopians, in their leopard skins and lion skins, carried long bows made of palm-wood – as much as six feet long – which were used to shoot small cane arrows tipped not with iron but with stone worked to a fine point, like the stone they use for engraving seals. They also had spears with spearheads of antelope horn, and knotted clubs. When going to battle they smeared half their bodies with chalk and half with vermilion. The Arabians and the Ethiopians from the country south of Egypt were commanded by Arsames, the son of Darius – his mother was Cyrus' daughter Artystone, the favourite wife of Darius, who had a statue made of her in beaten gold.

The eastern Ethiopians – for there were two sorts of Ethiopians in the army – served with the Indians. These were just like the southern Ethiopians, except for their language and their hair: their hair is straight, while that of the Ethiopians in Libya is the crispest and curliest in the world. The equipment of the Ethiopians from Asia was in most respects like the Indian, except that they wore headdresses consisting of horses' scalps, stripped off with the ears and mane attached – the ears were made to stand erect and the mane served as a crest. For shields they used the skins of cranes.

The Libyans were clothed in leather and carried javelins hardened with fire. Their commander was Massages, the son of Oarizus. The Paphlagonians wore wicker helmets, small shields, fairly short spears, javelins, and daggers. They wore the native high boot reaching halfway to the knee. Similarly equipped were the Ligyans, Matieni, Mariandynians, and Syrians (or Cappadocians, as the Persians call them). In command of the Paphlagonians and Matieni was Dotus, the son of Megasidrus, and in command of the Mariandynians, Ligyans, and Syrians was Gobryas, the son of Darius and Artystone.

The dress of the Phrygians was, with a few small differences, like the Paphlagonian. This people, according to the Macedonian account, were known as Briges during the period when they were Europeans and lived in Macedonia, and changed their name at the same time as, by migrating to Asia, they changed their country. The Armenians, who are Phrygian colonists, were armed in the Phrygian fashion and both contingents were commanded by Artochmes, the husband of one of Darius' daughters.

The Lydian equipment closely resembled the Greek. These people were known anciently as Maeonians, and took their present name from Lydus, the son of Atys. The Mysians wore the native helmet and were armed with small shields and javelins made of wood hardened in fire. They are Lydian colonists, and are known as Olympieni after Mt Olympus. The two latter contingents were led by Artaphernes, son of the same Artaphernes who landed with Datis at Marathon.

The Thracian troops wore fox skins as a headdress, tunics with the *zeira*, or long cloak, in this case brightly coloured, thrown over them, and high fawnskin boots; their weapons were the javelin, light shield, and small dagger. The Thracians after their migration to Asia became known as Bithynians; previously, according to their own account, they were called Strymonians, after the river Strymon upon which they lived, and from which they were driven by the Teucrians and Mysians.

The commander of these Asiatic Thracians was Bassaces, the son of Artabanus.

The Pisidians carried little ox-hide shields and a pair of hunting-spears of Lycian workmanship, and wore bronze helmets, crested, and decorated with the ears and horns of an ox, also in bronze. Their legs were bound with strips of crimson cloth. In the country where these people live there is an oracle of Ares.

The Cabalians (who are really Maeonians but are known as Lasonians) had the same kind of equipment as the Cilicians – I will describe it when I come to the Cilicians in the course of this catalogue. The Milyans carried short spears and had their clothes fastened with brooches; some of them were also armed with Lycian bows and wore leather casques. All these troops were led by Badres, the son of Hystanes.

The Moschians had wooden helmets and were armed with shields and short spears with long heads. Similarly equipped were the Tibareni, Macrones, and Mossynoeci; the officers who organized and commanded these troops were, for the two former, Ariomardus, the son of Darius and Parmys (who was daughter of Smerdis and granddaughter of Cyrus), and, for the two latter, Artaÿctes, the son of Cherasmis, governor of Sestos on the Hellespont.

The Marians wore the peculiar plaited helmets of their country and were armed with little leather shields and javelins; the Colchians had wooden helmets, small shields made of rawhide, short spears, and swords. These two contingents were under the command of Pharandates, the son of Teaspis. Similarly armed were the Alarodians and Saspires, under Masistius, the son of

Siromitras. The troops from the islands in the Persian Gulf (the islands, that is, where the Persian king settles people he has expelled from their homes) were dressed and armed very much in the Median fashion, and were commanded by Bagaeus' son Mardontes, who in the following year held a command at Mycale and was killed in the battle.

Such, then, were the troops of the various nations which made up the infantry. The names of their chief commanders I have already recorded; it was they who organized and numbered the troops, and appointed the commanders of thousands and myriads of men. The latter were responsible for appointing men to take charge of small units – squads of ten or a hundred. There were also other officers commanding contingents and nations, but those whom I mentioned above were the commanders.

Over them, and in general command of the infantry, were Mardonius, the son of Gobryas, Tritantaechmes, the son of Artabanus (the man who voted against the campaign), Smerdomenes, the son of Otanes (both nephews of Darius and Xerxes' cousins), Masistes, the son of Darius and Atossa, Gergis, the son of Ariazus, and Megabyzus, the son of Zopyrus. These six commanded all the infantry except the Ten Thousand – a body of picked Persian troops under the leadership of Hydarnes, the son of Hydarnes. This corps was known as the Immortals, because it was invariably kept up to strength; if a man was killed or fell sick, the vacancy he left was at once filled, so that its strength was never more nor less than 10,000.

Of all the troops in the army the native Persians were not only the best but also the most magnificently equipped; their dress and armour I have mentioned already, but should add that every man glittered with the gold which he carried about his person in unlimited quantity. They were accompanied, moreover, by covered carriages containing their women and servants, all elaborately fitted out. Special food, separate from that of the rest of the army, was brought along for them on camels and mules.

The nations above mentioned use cavalry, but for this expedition only the following provided it: first the Persians – armed in the same way as their infantry, except that some of them wore devices of hammered bronze or iron on their heads. Secondly, a nomad tribe called Sagartians, a people who speak Persian and dress in a manner half Persian, half Pactyan: these furnished a contingent 8000 strong. Their custom is to carry no weapons of bronze or iron except daggers; the special weapon upon which they chiefly rely is the lasso made of plaited strips of hide. In action, the moment they are in contact with the enemy, they throw their lassos, which have a noose at the end, and haul towards them whatever they catch, horse or man. The victim, tied up and helpless, is then dispatched. The Sagartian contingent was attached to the Persian. The Medes and Cissians were equipped like their infantry. The Indians, also armed like the Indian foot, rode, some on horseback, some in chariots drawn by either horses or wild asses. The Bactrians and Caspians were equipped like their infantry.

The Libyans were like their infantry in equipment, but all riding in chariots. The Caspeirians and Paricanians again had the same arms as their infantry. The Arabians, equipped like their infantry, rode camels, which in speed are not inferior to horses.

These were the only nations which provided cavalry, and the total strength, not counting camels and chariots, was 80,000. The cavalry was drawn up in squadrons, and the Arabian contingent brought up the rear to avoid spreading panic amongst the horses, who cannot endure the presence of camels.

In command of the cavalry were Datis' two sons, Harmamithras and Tithaeus. The third general of cavalry, Pharnuches, had been sick and left behind in Sardis. When the army was leaving Sardis, he met with an unhappy accident: a dog ran under his horse's feet, and the horse, taken by surprise, reared and threw its rider. As a result of the fall Pharnuches began to spit blood; and his sickness finally turned to consumption. His servants at once dealt with the horse according to his orders – bringing him to the spot where he had thrown his master, and cutting his legs off at the knees. So Pharnuches was relieved of his command.

The fleet, apart from transport vessels, consisted of 1207 triremes. They were furnished as follows:

The Phoenicians, with the Syrians of Palestine, contributed 300. The crews wore helmets very like the Greek ones, and linen corslets; they were armed with rimless shields and javelins. These people have a tradition that in ancient times they lived on the Persian Gulf, but migrated to the Syrian coast, where they are found today. This part of Syria, together with the country which extends southward to Egypt, is all known as Palestine.

The Egyptians contributed 200. They wore reticulated helmets and were armed with concave, broad-rimmed shields, boarding-spears, and heavy axes. Most of the crews wore corslets and carried long knives.

The Cyprians contributed 150. Their princes wore turbans, the common sailors peaked hats. The rest of their equipment resembled the Greek. According to the Cyprians' own account, some of them came originally from Salamis and Athens, some from Arcadia, some from Cythnus, some from Phoenicia and Ethiopia.

The Cilicians contributed 100. The crews wore the native helmet and woollen corslets and carried light rawhide shields. Each man was armed with two javelins and a sword which closely resembled the Egyptian long knife.

The ancient name of the Cilicians was Hypachaei; their present name they took from Cilix, the son of Agenor, a Phoenician.

The Pamphylians contributed 30. Their armour was Greek. These people are descended from the Greeks who followed Amphilochus and Calchas when the army was dispersed after the capture of Troy.

The Lycians contributed 50. They wore greaves and corslets; they carried bows of cornel-wood, cane arrows without feathers, and javelins. They had goatskins slung round their shoulders, and hats stuck round with feathers. They also carried daggers and riphooks. The Lycians are of Cretan origin; their old name was

Termilae, and they took their present one from Lycus son of Pandion, an Athenian.

The Asiatic Dorians contributed 30. Coming originally from the Peloponnese, they were armed in the Greek fashion.

The Carians contributed 70. Their equipment was similar to the Greek, except that they carried riphooks and daggers. Their old name I have already mentioned in an early chapter of this history.

The Ionians contributed 100. Their equipment was Greek. These people, according to the Greek account, as long as they lived in what is now known as Achaea in the Peloponnese, before the coming of Danaus and Xuthus, were called Pelasgians of the Coast. They took their present name from Xuthus' son Ion.

The islanders – also wearing Greek armour – contributed 17. They, too, are a Pelasgian people; they were later known as Ionians for the same reason as those who inhabited the twelve cities founded from Athens.

The Aeolians (also, as the Greeks suppose, originally a Pelasgian people) contributed 60. Their equipment was Greek.

The towns on the Hellespont and Bosphorus (the people in these places are Ionian and Dorian colonists) contributed 100 – all furnished with Greek equipment and armour. Abydos, however, was not included: the men of this town had orders from Xerxes to stay at home and guard the bridges.

All the ships also carried Persians, Medes, or Sacae as marines. The fastest ships were the Phoenician – and of these the Sidonian were the best. The men who served with the fleet like those who served with the army had their own native officers; but, as my story does not require it, I do not propose to mention their names. Some of them were far from distinguished, and every nation had as many officers as it had towns. In any case, these native officers were not really commanders; like the rest of the troops, they merely served as slaves. The names of the Persian generals who had the real command and were at the head of the contingents sent by the various nations, I have already recorded.

The naval commanders were as follows: Ariabignes son of Darius; Prexaspes son of Aspathines; Megabazus son of Megabates; Achaemenes son of Darius. Ariabignes, who was Darius' son by a daughter of Gobryas, commanded the Ionian and Carian contingent, Achaemenes, who was Xerxes' brother by both parents, the Egyptian. The rest of the fleet was under the other two. Galleys of thirty and fifty oars, horse-transports, and boats made the total number of the fleet up to 3000.

Next to the commanders the following were the best known of those who sailed with the fleet: Tetramnestus son of Anysus, from Sidon; Matten son of Siromus, from Tyre; Merbalus son of Agbalus, from Aradus; Syennesis son of Oromedon, from Cilicia; Cyberniscus son of Sicas, from Lycia; Gorgus son of Chersis and Timonax son of Timagoras, from Cyprus; and Histiaeus son of Tymnes, Pigres son of Hysseldomus, and Damasithymus son of Candaules, from Caria.

There is no need for me to mention all the other subordinate officers, but there is one name which I cannot omit – that of Artemisia. It seems to me a marvel that she – a woman – should have taken part in the campaign against Greece. On the death of her husband the tyranny had passed into her hands, and she sailed with the fleet in spite of the fact that she had a grown-up son and that there was consequently no necessity for her to do so. Her own spirit of adventure and manly courage were her only incentives. She was the daughter of Lygdamis, a Halicarnassian; on her mother's side she was Cretan. She sailed in command of the men of Halicarnassus, Cos, Nisyra, and Calydna, and furnished five ships of war. They were the most famous in the fleet, after the contingent from Sidon, and not one of the confederate commanders gave Xerxes sounder advice than she did. The places I mentioned as being under her rule are all Dorian – the Halicarnassians being colonists from Troezen, and the rest from Epidaurus.

I have now finished what I had to say about the fleet.

When the counting and marshalling of the troops had been completed, Xerxes thought he would like to hold a general review. Accordingly he drove in his chariot past the contingents of all the various nations, asking questions, the answers to which were taken down by his secretaries, until he had gone from one end of the army to the other, both horse and foot. Next the ships were launched, and Xerxes dismounting from his chariot went aboard a Sidonian vessel, where he took his seat under a canopy of gold and sailed along the line of the anchored fleet, asking questions about each ship and having the answers recorded, just as he had done with the army. The ships' masters had taken their vessels some four hundred feet from the beach, and brought up there in a single line with the bows turned shoreward and the fighting men drawn up on deck fully armed as for war. To hold his review, Xerxes passed along between the line and the shore.

Having sailed from one end to the other of the line of anchored ships, Xerxes went ashore again and sent for Demaratus, the son of Ariston, who was accompanying him in the march to Greece. 'Demaratus,' he said, 'it would give me pleasure at this point to put to you a few questions. You are a Greek, and a native, moreover, of by no means the meanest or weakest city in that country – as I learn not only from yourself but from the other Greeks I have spoken with. Tell me, then – will the Greeks dare to lift a hand against me? My own belief is that all the Greeks and all the other western peoples gathered together would be insufficient to withstand the attack of my army – and still more so if they are not united. But it is your opinion upon this subject that I should like to hear.'

'King,' Demaratus replied, 'is it a true answer you would like, or a pleasant one?'

'Tell me the truth,' said the king, 'and I promise that you will not suffer by it.' Encouraged by this Demaratus continued: 'My lord, you bid me speak nothing but the truth, to say nothing which might later be proved a lie. Very well then; this is my answer: poverty is Greece's inheritance from of old, but valour she won for herself by wisdom and the strength of law. By her valour Greece now keeps both poverty and despotism at bay.

'I think highly of all Greeks of the Dorian lands, but what I am about to say will apply not to all Dorians, but to the Spartans only. First then, they will not under any circumstances accept terms from you which would mean slavery for Greece; secondly, they will fight you even if the rest of Greece submits. Moreover, there is no use in asking if their numbers are adequate to enable them to do this; suppose a thousand of them take the field – then that thousand will fight you; and so will any number, greater than this or less.'

Xerxes laughed. 'Demaratus,' he exclaimed, 'what an extraordinary thing to say! Do you really suppose a thousand men would fight an army like mine? Now tell me, would *you* who were once, as you say, king of these people, be willing at this moment to fight ten men single-handed? And yet, if things in Sparta are really as you have described them, then, according to your laws, you as king ought to take on a double share – so that if every Spartan is a match for ten men of mine, I should expect you to be a match for twenty. Only in that way can you prove the truth of your claim. But if you Greeks, who think so much of yourselves, are all of the size and quality of those I have spoken with when they have visited my court – and of yourself, Demaratus – there is some danger of your words being nothing but an empty boast. But let me put my point as reasonably as I can – how is it possible that a thousand men, or ten thousand, or fifty thousand, should stand up to an army as big as mine, especially if they were not under a single master, but all perfectly free to do as they pleased? Suppose them to have five thousand men: in that case we should be more than a thousand to one! If, like ours, their troops were subject to the control of a single man, then possibly for fear of him, in spite of the disparity in numbers, they might show some sort of factitious courage, or let themselves be whipped into battle; but, as every man is free to follow his fancy, it is not conceivable that they should do either. Indeed, my own opinion is that even on equal terms the Greeks could hardly face the Persians alone. We, too, have this thing that you were speaking of – I do not say it is common, but it does exist; for instance, amongst the Persians in my bodyguard there are men who would willingly fight with three Greeks together. But you know nothing of such things, or you could not talk such nonsense.'

'King,' Demaratus answered, 'I knew before I began that if I spoke the truth you would not like it. But, as you demanded the plain truth and nothing less, I told you how things are with the Spartans. Yet you are well aware that I now feel but little affection for my countrymen, who robbed me of my hereditary power and privileges and made me a fugitive without a home – whereas your father welcomed me at his court and gave me the means of livelihood and somewhere to live. Surely it is unreasonable to reject kindness; any sensible man will cherish it. Personally I do not claim to be able to fight ten men – or two; indeed I should prefer not even to fight with one. But should it be necessary – should there be some great cause to urge me on – then nothing would give me more pleasure than to stand up to one of those men of yours who claim to be a match for three Greeks. So it is with the Spartans; fighting singly, they are as good as any, but fighting together they are the best soldiers in the world. They are free –

yes – but not entirely free; for they have a master, and that master is Law, which they fear much more than your subjects fear you. Whatever this master commands, they do; and his command never varies: it is never to retreat in battle, however great the odds, but always to remain in formation, and to conquer or die. If, my lord, you think that what I have said is nonsense – very well; I am willing henceforward to hold my tongue. This time I spoke because you forced me to speak. In any case, I pray that all may turn out as you desire.'

Xerxes burst out laughing at Demaratus' answer, and good-humouredly let him go.

After the conversation, Xerxes appointed Mascames, son of Megadostes, to the governorship of Doriscus in place of the man who had been given that post by Darius, and then continued his march through Thrace towards Greece. Mascames was later to prove himself a very remarkable person; so much so, in fact, that Xerxes used to send a special present every year in recognition of his superiority to all the governors appointed either by himself or by Darius; moreover his son Artaxerxes showed the same favour to Mascames' descendants. Persian governors had held posts in Thrace and on the Hellespont before Xerxes' expedition, but in the years which succeeded it all of them except the governor of Doriscus were driven out by the Greeks – Mascames no one was able to expel, though many tried to do so. This is the reason for the annual present from the Persian king. Of the governors who were expelled by the Greeks the only one whom Xerxes considered as a man of any worth was Boges, governor of Eion. Boges he was never tired of praising, and those of his sons who were left in Persia and survived him he treated with marked respect. This man did, indeed, deserve the highest praise; for when he was besieged by the Athenians under Cimon, son of Miltiades, and the chance was offered him of leaving the town under treaty and returning to Asia, he refused to do so, because he was afraid the king might think that he had shirked his duty to save his skin; so, rather than surrender, he held out to the last extremity. When all supplies were consumed, he made a huge pile of timber, set it on fire, and then, cutting the throats of his children, wife, concubines, and servants, flung their bodies into the flames; then he collected all the gold and silver in the town, scattered it broadcast from the walls into the Strymon, and ended by leaping into the fire himself. For this behaviour his name is still mentioned in Persia with respect; and it is right that it should be.

From Doriscus Xerxes marched on towards Greece, pressing into his service the men of every nation which lay in his path; for, as I have already recorded, the whole country as far as Thessaly had been forced into subjection and made tributary to Persia by the conquests, first, of Megabazus and, later, of Mardonius, After leaving Doriscus the army passed first by the Samothracian forts, the most westerly of which is Mesembria; the next place is Stryme, a town belonging to the Thasians. Between the two runs the Lisus, a stream which on that occasion failed to provide sufficient water for Xerxes' army. It was drunk dry. This part of the country was once called Gallaica instead of its present name of Briantica; strictly, however, it too belongs to the Cicones. Having crossed the dried-up channel of the Lisus, Xerxes moved on past the Greek towns of Maronia, Dicaea, and Abdera, passing also some well-known lakes in that neighbourhood, namely Ismaris, between Maronia and Stryme, and Bistonis near Dicaea, a lake into which flow the rivers Trauos and Compsatus. At Abdera there was not, to be sure, any well-known lake for him to pass, but he crossed the river Nestus, which there enters the sea. Next he reached the settlements owned by the Thasians upon the continent, in one of which there is a lake about four miles in circumference, full of fish and very salty. It was drunk dry by the pack-animals alone. The town by this lake is called Pistyrus. All these Greek coastal settlements Xerxes kept on his left as he marched westward. The Thracian tribes lying along his route were the Paeti, Cicones, Bistones, Sapaei, Dersaei, Edoni, and Satrae; some of these lived on the coast and furnished ships for the king's fleet, but others lived inland, and of these all the tribes I have mentioned except the Satrae were forced to serve in the army. The Satrae, so far as we know, have never yet been reduced to subjection, and are the only Thracian people to have kept their independence right down to my day. The reason for this is the nature of their country, which consists of high mountains, thickly wooded with timber of all sorts and covered with snow. They are also first-rate fighters. It is in the territory of this people that there is the oracle of Dionysus, situated on the loftiest mountain range. The service of the temple belongs to the Bessi, a branch of the Satrae; and there is a Priestess, as at Delphi, to deliver the oracles – which, by the way, are not more complicated than the Delphic.

Once through the region mentioned above, Xerxes next passed the Pierian forts, one of which is called Phagres and another Pergamus. His route led him close by the walls, as he kept on his right the great range of Pangaeum, where there are gold and silver mines worked partly by the Pierians and Odomanti but mostly by the Satrae. Then he passed through the country of the Doberes and Paeoplae (Paeonian tribes living north of Pangaeum), and continued in a westerly direction as far as the Strymon and the town of Eion, where Boges, whom I mentioned just now, was governor during his lifetime. The country in the neighbourhood of Mt Pangaeum is known as Phyllis; it extends westward to the Angites, a stream which flows into the Strymon, and southward as far as the Strymon itself. This latter river the Magi tried to propitiate by a sacrifice of white horses, and after performing many other magical tricks in the hope of winning the river's favour, they crossed it by the bridges which they found at Nine Ways, a place in the territory of the Edoni; and when they learnt that Nine Ways was the name of the place, they took nine native boys and nine girls and buried them alive there. Burying people alive is a Persian custom; I understand that Xerxes' wife Amestris in her old age did it to fourteen Persian boys of distinguished family, by way of a present which she hoped the supposed god of the underworld would accept instead of herself.

From the Strymon the army came to a strip of coast running westward, on which stands the Greek town of Argilus. The country here, and for some distance inland, is called Bisaltia. Thence, keeping the Gulf of Posidium on his left, Xerxes marched through the plain of Syleus, past the Greek town of Stagirus, until he arrived at Acanthus. Like the others whom I mentioned before, the inhabitants of these places and of the country round Mt Pangaeum were pressed into his service, those on the coast being forced to sail with the fleet, those inland to march with the army. The road which King Xerxes took remains untouched to my day; the Thracians hold it in profound reverence and never plough it up or sow crops on it.

At Acanthus Xerxes issued a proclamation of friendship to the people and made them a present of a suit of Median clothes, with many expressions of approval for their enthusiastic support of the war and for the work they had done on the canal. It was while Xerxes was here that Artachaees fell sick and died. He was a man of the Achaemenid family, much respected by Xerxes, and had been in charge of the construction of the canal. He was the biggest man in Persia – about 8 ft 2 ins. high – and had the loudest voice in the world, so that Xerxes was greatly distressed at his death and had him carried out and buried with all pomp and ceremony. The whole army helped to raise a mound over his grave. The people of Acanthus, in obedience to an oracle, offer sacrifice to Artachaees, as to a hero, and call upon his name in prayer.

The death of Artachaees was, as I said, very distressing for Xerxes; but things were even worse for the Greeks who had to entertain the Persian army and provide a dinner for the king. They were utterly ruined, and were obliged to leave house and home. For instance, when the Thasians, on behalf of their towns on the mainland, billeted and fed the army, Antipater, the son of Orgeus, a citizen of the highest repute, to whom the arrangements had been entrusted, proved that the meal cost 400 talents of silver. And similar accounts were returned by the officers in the other towns. A great deal of fuss had been made about the meal, and orders for its preparation had been issued a long time in advance; accordingly, the moment that word came from the officers who carried the king's commands, people in every town distributed their stores of grain and employed themselves for months on end in making barely and wheat flour, in buying up and fattening the best cattle they could find, and feeding poultry in coops and waterfowl in ponds, to be ready for the army when it came. In addition to this they ordered the manufacture of drinking cups and mixing-bowls of gold and silver, and of everything else that is needed to adorn the table. All this, of course, was for the king himself and those who dined with him; for the troops in general the preparations were confined to food. On the arrival of the army, there was always a tent ready for Xerxes to take his rest in, while the men bivouacked in the open; but it was when dinner-time came that the real trouble for the unfortunate hosts began. The guests ate their fill and, after spending the night in the place, pulled up the tent next morning, seized the cups and table-gear and everything else it contained, and marched off without leaving a single thing behind. A man of Abdera called Megacreon spoke to the point on this subject, when he advised all the people of the town to take their wives to the temples and pray heaven to continue to spare them one half of their troubles, with proper gratitude for the blessing already received, that King Xerxes was not in the habit of taking *two* dinners a day. It was clear enough that if the orders had been to prepare a morning meal as well as an evening one, the people of Abdera would have had to clear out altogether before Xerxes arrived, or else be hopelessly crushed by the burden of the expense. Nevertheless the various places along the route did manage to carry out their orders, though not without severe suffering.

At Acanthus Xerxes sent the fleet on separately, and ordered the commanders to wait for him at Therma – the town on the gulf to which it has given its name. It was through Therma that he had ascertained his shortest route to lie. From Doriscus to Acanthus the army had been marching in three divisions, of which one under Mardonius and Masistes took the coast road and kept in close touch with the fleet, another under Tritantaechmes and Gergis a parallel route some distance inland, and the third under Smerdomenes and Megabyzus a route between the two. This third division Xerxes himself accompanied.

Having received from Xerxes its orders to proceed, the fleet passed through the Athos canal, which led to the deep bight on which stand the towns of Assa, Pilorus, Singus, and Sarte; from all these places reinforcements were taken on board, and a course was set for the Gulf of Therma. Rounding Ampelus, the promontory in Torone, they sailed past the Greek towns of Torone, Galepsus, Sermyle, Mecyberna, and Olynthus (the country round here is known as Sithonia), levying more ships and men; but the main body of the fleet sailed direct from Cape Ampelus to Canastraeum (the southernmost point of Pallene), and then took over more reinforcements in both ships and men from Potidaea, Aphytis, Nea, Aege, Therambos, Scione, Mende, and Sane – all towns in what is now called Pallene, but used to be called Phlegra. From here they continued to follow the coast towards the rendezvous at Therma, taking over on the way more men from the towns near Pallene and the Thermaic Gulf – namely Lipaxus, Combreia, Lisae, Gigonus, Campsa, Smila, and Aeneia. All this region is still known as Crossaea. After passing the last of these towns – Aeneia – the fleet found itself off Mygdonia and actually within the gulf, and proceeded to the rendezvous at Therma. The ships also called at Sindus and Chalestra on the river Axius, which forms the boundary between Mygdonia and Bottiaeis. This latter district has a small strip of coastline, occupied by the towns of Ichanae and Pella.

While the fleet waited near Therma and the Axius and the intervening towns, Xerxes with the army was on his way from Acanthus by the inland road to the rendezvous. He passed through Paeonia and Crestonia to the river Echeidorus, which rises in the latter country and flows through Mygdonia, to reach the sea by way of the marshland at the mouth of the Axius. It was during this march that his pack-camels were attacked by lions, which came down from their haunts at night and never attacked either the men or any of the other animals, but only the camels. I marvel at what it could have been that made the lions ignore every other living creature and set only upon the camels – beasts which they had never seen, or had any experience of before. This part of the country – namely the region between the river Nestus which runs through Abdera and the Achelous which runs through Acarnania – abounds with lions, and also with wild oxen, which have those enormous horns that are imported into Greece. One would see no lions anywhere in Europe east of the Nestus, or in the continent west of the Achelous; they exist only in the country between those rivers.

At Therma Xerxes halted his army, and the troops went into camp. They occupied the whole seaboard from Therma in Mygdonia to the Lydias and Haliacmon – two rivers which unite and form the boundary between Bottiaeis and Macedonia. While they were encamped here, all the rivers I have mentioned supplied enough water for their needs except the Echeidorus, which failed.

Xerxes could see from Therma the Thessalian mountains – the towering peaks of Olympus and Ossa – and on being informed that between the two mountains there was a narrow gorge through which the river Peneus ran, and also a road leading into Thessaly, he suddenly felt that he would like to go by sea and inspect the mouth of the river. His intention was to take the army by the upper road through the inland parts of Macedonia into Perrhaebia, past the town of Gonnus; for that, he heard, was the safest route. No sooner, therefore, had the fancy taken him than he acted upon it; and going aboard the Sidonian vessel which he always used for any such occasion, he gave the signal to the rest of the fleet to put to sea, leaving the army behind in its encampments. The appearance of the river-mouth, on his arrival there, was a great marvel to him, so that he called the guides and asked them if it was possible to turn the course of the river so as to bring it to the sea at some other point. Now it is said that in the remote past Thessaly was a lake – a not unreasonable supposition, as the whole country is enclosed by lofty hills. To the eastward is the great barrier of Pélion and Ossa, two mountains whose bases form a continuous chain; then there is the range of Olympus on the north, Pindus on the west, and Othrys on the south. In the centre of this ring of mountains lies the low plain of Thessaly. A number of rivers pour their waters into it, the best known being the Peneus, Apidanus, Onochonus, Enipeus, and Pamisus; all these flow down from the surrounding mountains, unite into a single stream, and find their way to the sea through one narrow gorge. After the junction the other names are all dropped and the river is known simply as the Peneus. The story then is that, ages ago, before the gorge existed and while there was as yet no outlet for the water, these rivers, though, like Lake Boebeis, they had yet no names, poured down from the hills as much water as they do today, and so made Thessaly an inland sea. The natives of Thessaly have a tradition that the gorge which forms the outlet for the river was made by Poseidon, and the story is a reasonable one; for if one believes that it is Poseidon who shakes the earth and that chasms caused by earthquake are attributable to him, then the mere sight of this place would be enough to make one say that it is Poseidon's handiwork. It certainly appeared to me that the cleft in the mountains had been caused by an earthquake.

So when Xerxes asked if there was any other outlet by which the Peneus could reach the sea, the guides, who were perfectly familiar with the facts, replied, 'No, my lord; there is no other outlet but this, because the whole of Thessaly is surrounded with a ring of mountains, like a crown.' At this Xerxes is said to have remarked: 'The Thessalians are wise men; it was with this very danger in view that they made their submission to me in good time – they realized, amongst other things, that their country is easy to take and very vulnerable. Nothing more would have been needed than to flood the country by damming the gorge, and so forcing the river from its present channel; that would have put all Thessaly except the mountains under water.' In saying this he had, of course, the Aleuadae in mind – the Thessalian family who were the first Greeks to submit to the Persian king. Doubtless he thought that they had made the offer of friendship in the name of the people generally.

Then, having seen the place, and having made this comment, Xerxes returned by sea to Therma.

His stay in Pieria lasted a number of days, during which one third of his army was felling the forest through the mountains of Macedonia, making a route for his troops to follow into Perrhaebia. Meanwhile the representatives who had been sent to Greece to demand submission rejoined the army – some empty-handed, others bringing the earth and water. Those who gave the tokens of submission were the following: the Thessalians,

Dolopes, Aenianes, Perrhaebi, Locrians, Magnetes, Malians, Achaeans of Phthiotis, Thebans, and all the other Boeotians except the people of Plataea and Thespiae. Against these the Greeks who determined to resist the invader swore an oath to the effect that, once the war was fought to a successful conclusion, they would punish all men of Greek blood, who without compulsion yielded to the Persians, and dedicate a tenth part of their property to the god at Delphi.

To Athens and Sparta Xerxes sent no demand for submission because of what happened to the messengers whom Darius had sent on a previous occasion: at Athens they were thrown into the pit like criminals, at Sparta they were pushed into a well – and told that if they wanted earth and water for the king, to get them from there. This time, therefore, Xerxes refrained from sending a request. Just what disagreeable consequences were suffered by the Athenians for this treatment of the king's messengers, I am unable to say; perhaps it was the destruction of their city and the countryside around it – though I do not myself believe that this happened as a direct result of their crime. The case is clear, however, with respect to the Spartans: upon them fell the anger of Agamemnon's herald Talthybius. There is in Sparta a temple dedicated to Talthybius, and a family – the Talthybiadae – descended from him, which enjoys the sole privilege of holding the office of herald. Now there was a long period after the incident I have mentioned above, during which the Spartans were unable to obtain favourable signs from their sacrifices; this caused them deep concern, and they held frequent assemblies at which the question 'Is there any Spartan who is willing to die for his country?' was put by the public crier. Thereupon two Spartans, Sperchias, the son of Aneristus, and Bulis, the son of Nicoles, both men of good family and great wealth, volunteered to offer their lives to Xerxes in atonement for Darius' messengers who had been killed in Sparta. They were dispatched accordingly to Persia to meet their doom. The courage of these two men is indeed admirable, and what they said is no less so. On their way to Susa they visited Hydarnes, a Persian by birth who was in command of the whole Asiatic sea-board; and by him they were given a hospitable welcome and invited to dinner. During the meal Hydarnes said: 'Why is it, Lacedaemonians, that you refuse to be friends with the king? You have only to look at me and the position I enjoy to see that he knows how to reward merit. Now Xerxes believes that you, too, are men of merit; and both of you, if only you would submit, might find yourselves in authority over lands in Greece which he would give you.'

'Hydarnes,' came the answer, 'the advice you give us does not spring from a full knowledge of the situation. You know one half of what is involved, but not the other half. You understand well enough what slavery is, but freedom you have never experienced, so you do not know if it tastes sweet or bitter. If you ever did come to experience it, you would advise us to fight for it not with spears only, but with axes too.'

After this they continued their journey to Susa, and the first thing that happened when they entered the presence of the king was that the men of the royal bodyguard ordered – and, indeed, attempted to compel – them to bow down to the ground in the act of worship. The two Spartans, however, declared that they would never do such a thing, even though the guards should push their heads down on to the floor. It was not, they said, the custom in Sparta to worship a mere man like themselves, and it was not for that purpose that they had come to Persia. So they persisted in their refusal, adding words to the following effect: 'King of the Medes, the Spartans sent us here to suffer punishment in reparation for the murder of the Persian messengers in Sparta'; to which Xerxes with truly noble generosity replied that he would not behave like the Spartans, who by murdering the ambassadors of a foreign power had broken the law which all the world holds sacred. He had no intention of doing the very thing for which he blamed them, or, by taking reprisals, of freeing the Spartans from the burden of their crime.

This conduct on the part of the Spartans succeeded for a time in allaying the anger of Talthybius, in spite of the fact that Sperchias and Bulis returned home alive; long afterwards, however, during the war between Athens and the Peloponnese, the Spartans believe that it was aroused again – and in this, I think, the hand of God was clearly to be seen. That Talthybius' anger should have fallen upon *ambassadors*, and should not have ceased until it was fully satisfied, was only just; but that it should have struck the sons of the very men who visited the Persian king because of it – that the objects of it should have been Bulis' son Nicolaus and Sperchias' son Aneristus, the same man who took Halieis, a Tirynthian colony, with a merchant ship and an armed crew – this, to me at least, is clear evidence of divine intervention. What happened was that these two men were sent by the Spartans on a mission to Asia and were betrayed by Sitalces son of Teres, the king of Thrace, and by Nymphodorus son of Pythes, a native of Abdera; they were made prisoners at Bisanthe on the Hellespont and taken to Attica, where they were put to death by the Athenians in company with Aristeas son of Adeimantus, of Corinth. This, however, took place long after Xerxes' invasion of Greece, and I must get back to my story.

The purpose of Xerxes' expedition, which was directed nominally against Athens, was in fact the conquest of the whole of Greece. The various Greek communities had long been aware of this, but they viewed the coming danger with very different eyes. Some had already made their submission, and were consequently in good spirits, because they were sure of getting off lightly at the invaders' hands; others, who had refused to submit, were thrown into panic partly because there were not enough ships in Greece to meet the Persians with any chance of success, and partly because most of the Greeks were unwilling to fight and all too ready to accept Persian dominion. At this point I find myself compelled to express an opinion which I know most people will object to; nevertheless, as I believe it to be true, I will not suppress it. If the Athenians, through fear of the approaching danger, had abandoned their country, or if they had stayed there and submitted to Xerxes, there would have been no attempt to resist the Persians by sea; and, in the absence of a Greek fleet, it is easy to see what would have been the course of events on land. However many lines of fortification the Spartans had built across the Isthmus, they would have been deserted by their confederates; not that their allies would have willingly deserted them, but they could not have helped doing so, because one by one they would have fallen victims to the Persian naval power. Thus the Spartans would have been left alone – to perform great deeds and to die nobly. Or, on the other hand, it is possible that before things came to the ultimate test, the sight of the rest of Greece submitting to Persia might have driven them to make terms with Xerxes. In either case the Persian conquest of Greece would have been assured; for I cannot myself see what possible use there could have been in fortifying the Isthmus, if the Persians had command of the sea. In view of this, therefore, one is surely right in saying that Greece was saved by the Athenians. It was the Athenians who held the balance: whichever side they joined was sure to prevail. It was the Athenians, too, who, having chosen that Greece should live and preserve her freedom, roused to battle the other Greek states which had not yet submitted. It was the Athenians who – after the gods – drove back the Persian king. Not even the terrifying warnings of the oracle at Delphi could persuade them to abandon Greece; they stood firm and had the courage to meet the invader.

[. . .]

At a conference of the Greek states who were loyal to the general cause, guarantees were exchanged, and the decision was reached that the first thing to be done was to patch up their own quarrels and stop any fighting which happened to be going on amongst members of the confederacy. There were a number of such disputes at the time, the most serious being the quarrel between Athens and Aegina. Having learnt that Xerxes and his army had reached Sardis, they next resolved to send spies into Asia to get information about the Persian forces; at the same time, in the hope of uniting, if it were possible, the whole Greek world and of bringing all the various communities to undertake joint action in face of the common danger, they decided to send an embassy to Argos to conclude an alliance, another to Gelon, the son of Deinomenes, in Sicily, and others, again, to Corcyra and Crete. Gelon was said to be very powerful – far more powerful than anyone else of Greek nationality.

These decisions were put into force at once. The private quarrels were settled, and three men sent off to Asia to collect information. They arrived in Sardis and found out all they could about the king's army, but were caught in the process, tortured by the Persian army commanders, and condemned to death. But when Xerxes was told that they were about to be executed, he disapproved of his generals' decision and sent men from his bodyguard with orders, if the three spies were still alive, to bring them before him. As the sentence had not yet been carried out, the spies were brought to the king, who, having satisfied himself about the reason for their presence in Sardis, instructed his guards to take them round and let them see the whole army, infantry and cavalry, and then, when they were satisfied that they had seen everything, to let them go without molestation to whatever country they pleased. After giving this order he explained the purpose of it by pointing out that, if the spies had been executed, the Greeks would not have been able to learn in good time how incalculably great the Persian strength was – and the killing of three men would not have done the enemy much harm; but if, on the other hand, the spies returned home, he was confident that their report on the magnitude of the Persian power would induce the Greeks to surrender their liberty before the actual invasion took place, so that there would be no need to go to the trouble of fighting a war at all. Xerxes had expressed a similar opinion on another occasion, when he was at Abydos and saw boats sailing down the Hellespont with cargoes of food from the Black Sea for Aegina and the Peloponnese. His counsellors, learning that they were enemy vessels, were prepared to seize them, and looked to the king for orders to do so. 'Where are they bound for?' Xerxes asked. 'To Persia's enemies, my lord,' came the answer, 'with a cargo of grain.' 'Well,' said the king, 'are we not bound ourselves for the same destination? And does not our equipment include grain amongst other things? I do not see that the men in those ships are doing us any harm in carrying our grain for us.' The three spies, then, after their tour of inspection, were allowed to return to Europe.

The Greeks who had united for resistance to Persia next dispatched their representatives to Argos. The Argives themselves explain their subsequent behaviour as follows: they were aware from the beginning of the Persian preparations against Greece, and knew very well that the Greeks would try to enlist their support in meeting the invasion; so they sent to Delphi for advice upon what action would, under the circumstances, be best for them to take. The reason for this step was the fact that six thousand of their men had recently been killed by the Spartans under Cleomenes, the son of Anaxandrides. The Priestess' answer to their question was this:

> Loathed by your neighbours, dear to the immortal gods,
> Hold your javelin within and sit upon your guard.
> Guard the head well, and the head will save the body.

This oracle had already been delivered, when the envoys arrived in Argos, and entered the council chamber to deliver their message. The Argive answer was, that they were willing to do what they were asked upon two conditions: first they must obtain a thirty years' truce with Sparta, and, secondly, share with Sparta, on equal terms, the command of the confederate forces. By right Argos was entitled to the sole command; nevertheless they would be content with an equal division.

Such, according to them, was their Council's answer, in spite of the fact that the oracle had forbidden them to join the confederacy. Moreover, though they shrank from disobeying the oracle, it was important to them to secure the thirty years' truce, to give their sons the chance of growing up during the period of peace; and if they failed to secure it, and were unlucky enough to suffer another defeat – this time at the hands of the Persians – it seemed only too likely that they would find themselves permanently subject to Sparta. The Spartan envoys replied to the demands of the Argive government by saying that they would refer the question of the truce to their people; on the other matter, however, namely the army command, they already had their instructions, and their answer was that Sparta had two kings and Argos only one, and it was not possible to deprive either of the Spartan kings of his command; on the other hand, there was nothing to prevent the Argive ruler from having one vote like each of the two Spartans.

The Argives add that they found the Spartan attitude intolerably grasping, and, rather than give way to it, they preferred to submit to foreign domination; accordingly they gave notice to the envoys that they must be out of the country before sunset, or be treated as enemies.

So much for the Argive account of this transaction; there is, however, another story current throughout Greece, to the effect that Xerxes sent a man to Argos before his army started on its march. 'Men of Argos,' this person is supposed to have said upon his arrival, 'King Xerxes has a message for you. We Persians believe that we are descended from Perses, whose father was Danae's son Perseus, and whose mother was Andromeda the daughter of Cepheus. Thus we are of the same blood as yourselves, and it would not be right for us to make war upon the people from whom we have sprung, any more than it would be right for you to help others by opposing us. Rather you should hold aloof from the coming struggle and take no part in it. If things turn out as I hope they will, there is no people I shall hold in greater esteem than you.'

The story goes on to say that the Argives were much impressed by Xerxes' message; they made no promises for the moment, and put forward no demand for a share in the command of the army; later, however, when the Greeks were trying to obtain their support, they did make the claim, because they knew that the Spartans would refuse to grant it, and that they would thus have an excuse for taking no part in the war. There are people in Greece who say that this account is borne out by a remark made long afterwards by Artaxerxes. Callias, the son of Hipponicus, and a number of other Athenians were in Susa, the city of Memnon, on different business, and it so happened that their visit coincided with that of some representatives from Argos, who had been sent to ask Xerxes' son Artaxerxes if the friendly relations, which the Argives had established with his father, still held good, or if they were now considered by Persia as enemies. 'They do indeed hold good,' Artaxerxes is said to have replied; 'there is no city which I believe to be a better friend to me than Argos.'

For my own part I cannot positively state that Xerxes either did; or did not, send the messenger to Argos; nor can I guarantee the story of the Argives going to Susa and asking Artaxerxes about their relationship with Persia. I express no opinion on this matter other than that of the Argives themselves. One thing, however, I am very sure of: and that is, that if all mankind agreed to meet, and everyone brought his own sufferings along with him for the purpose of exchanging them for somebody else's, there is not a man who, after taking a good look at his neighbour's sufferings, would not be only too happy to return home with his own. So the Argives were not the worst offenders. My business is to record what people say, but I am by no means bound to believe it – and that may be taken to apply to this book as a whole. There is yet another story about the Argives: it was they, according to some, who invited the Persians to invade Greece, because their war with Sparta was going badly and they felt that anything would be better than their present plight.

Another embassy was sent by the confederates to Sicily, to confer with Gelon. [. . .] Gelon himself was afraid that Greece would be unable to survive the Persian invasion; at the same time, as tyrant of Sicily, he could not bring himself to go to the Peloponnese and submit to taking orders from Spartans. Accordingly he chose a different course. As soon as news came that Xerxes was over the Hellespont, he sent three penteconters under the charge of Cadmus, the son of Scythes, a native of Cos, with instructions to go to Delphi, where, equipped with a large sum of money and plenty of friendly words, he was to wait and see how the war would go; then, if the Persians won, he was to give the money to Xerxes together with earth and water of Gelon's dominions. If the Greeks won, he was to bring the money back again.

Some time before this Cadmus had inherited the position of absolute master of Cos from his father, who had established his power there on firm foundations; yet of his own free will, without threat of violence from any quarter, he had, simply from his sense of justice, abdicated his power and handed it over to the people. He then left home for Sicily, where he took the town of

Zancle with the Samians – or Messene, as it was afterwards called – and lived there. This was how Cadmus
came to Sicily, and was the reason why Gelon, having
had evidence already of his sense of honour, chose him
for the mission to Delphi. And now yet another honest
action, perhaps the most remarkable of all, was to be
added to the former ones: having in his hands the large
sum of money which Gelon had entrusted to him, with
every opportunity of keeping it, he preferred not to; and
after the Greek victory, and the departure of Xerxes, he
returned to Sicily with the money intact.

There is a story in Sicily that Gelon would have sent
help to Greece in spite of the necessity of serving under
Spartan commanders had it not been for the action of
Terillus, the son of Crinippus and tyrant of Himera.
Driven from his home by Aenesidemus' son Theron, the
sole ruler of Agrigentum, he brought into Sicily just
about this time an army 300,000 strong, from Carthage,
Libya, Iberia, Liguria, Helisycia, Sardinia, and Corsica –
under the command of Hamilcar, the son of Hanno and
king of Carthage. Terillus had induced Hamilcar to bring
over this force partly by the friendship which existed
between them, but more particularly through the warm
support of Anaxilaus, the tyrant of Rhegium, the son of
Cretines; for Anaxilaus, who was married to Terillus'
daughter Cydippe, and wished to be of service to
his father-in-law, gave Hamilcar his own children as
hostages in order to persuade him to undertake the expedition. Under these circumstances, as it was impossible
for Gelon to give military aid to Greece, he sent the
money to Delphi. The Sicilians also maintain that the

victory of Gelon and Theron over Hamilcar of Carthage took place on the same day as the Greek victory over Persia at Salamis. Hamilcar was Carthaginian on his father's side only, for his mother came from Syracuse; he won the throne of Carthage by right of merit, and I have heard that during the battle, when things were beginning to go against him, he vanished. Gelon afterwards searched for him everywhere, but there was no trace of him, alive or dead. The tradition in Carthage – and it is probable – is that all the time the battle lasted, which was from dawn to late in the evening, Hamilcar remained in camp trying to obtain a favourable omen from sacrifices, burning whole carcasses on an immense fire; and at last, seeing, as he poured the wine upon the sacrificed victims, that his army was giving way, he leapt into the flames, was burnt to nothing, and in this way disappeared. But whatever explanation we adopt of his disappearance, the fact remains that the Carthaginians offer sacrifice to him, and monuments were erected to him in all their colonies in addition to the one – the most splendid of all – in Carthage itself. So ended the campaign in Sicily.

The envoys who went to Sicily called also at Corcyra and put their request for help in the same words as they used to Gelon. The immediate result was a promise from the Corcyraeans to send a fleet in support of the alliance. It was impossible, they said, to stand aside and see Greece overwhelmed; they must help her to the utmost of their power, because if she fell not a day would pass before they themselves were reduced to slavery. This answer sounded promising enough, but when the time came to act upon it, the Corcyraeans changed their minds; and having put into commission a fleet of sixty warships, they dawdled about before getting to sea, and then sailed only as far as the Peloponnese, where they hung round in the neighbourhood of Pylos and Taenarum, waiting, like Gelon, to see the result of the fighting. They thought it most unlikely that the Greeks would win; the Persians, in their opinion, would gain a complete victory and make themselves masters of all Greece. Their conduct was deliberately designed to enable them to say, in this event, to Xerxes that, though they might have answered the Greek appeal for aid by sending a fleet second in strength only to that of Athens, they had refused to do so, not wishing to oppose him or to take any action which he would not like. They hoped, no doubt, that this would get them better treatment than the other Greek states – and so, indeed, it would have done, I admit. They also had an excuse ready to offer to the Greeks – and used it when the time came and they were reproached for their failure to send assistance. The excuse was that they had fitted out sixty triremes, but had been prevented by prevailing north-easters from getting round Cape Malea: this explained their absence from the battle of Salamis – an absence in no way due to disloyalty or cowardice.

The Cretans, on the arrival of the Greek envoys with their appeal, sent to Delphi to inquire jointly whether or not it would be to their advantage to make common cause with Greece. 'Foolish men,' the oracle replied, 'do you not still resent all the tears which Minos in his anger caused you to weep after you helped Menelaus? Was he not angry because the Greeks did not help you to avenge his death at Camicus, whereas you did help them to avenge the rape by a foreign prince of a woman from Sparta?' When the Cretans heard that answer, they refrained from joining the alliance.

The story goes that Minos went to Sicania – or Sicily, as it is now called – in search of Daedalus, and there met a violent death. In course of time all the Cretans except the people of Polichna and Praesus, encouraged by the god, went with a large fleet to Sicania, where for five years they besieged Camicus – a town which in my day belonged to Agrigentum. Unable to take the place, or to continue the siege because of lack of provisions, they finally gave up and went away. In the course of their voyage they were caught by a violent storm off Iapygia and driven ashore, and, as their vessels were smashed up and they had no apparent means of getting back to Crete, they built for themselves the town of Hyria. Here they stayed, and instead of Cretans, became the mainland Iapygians of Messapia. From Hyria they founded the other towns which the people of Tarentum, long after, suffered such severe loss in attempting to overthrow; indeed, on that occasion there was, of all those we know, the worst slaughter of Greeks; not only the Tarentines were involved but the people of Rhegium as well, for they were compelled by Micythus the son of Choerus to support Tarentum and lost three thousand men. The losses of Tarentum were too many to count. Micythus had been a household servant of Anaxilaus and was left by him in charge of Rhegium. It was he who settled in Tegea in Arcadia after his expulsion from Rhegium and made the offering of all those well-known statues at Olympia. However, I must leave this digression about Rhegium and Tarentum and get back to my story.

According to the tradition in Praesus, men of various nationality, but especially Greeks, came to settle in Crete after it was depopulated by the expedition to Sicily; then in the third generation after the death of Minos came the Trojan war, in which the Cretans proved themselves by no means the most despicable champions of Menelaus; their reward for this service on their return home was famine and plague for both men and cattle, so that for the second time Crete was denuded of its population. Thus it happens that the present Cretans, together with the remnant of the former population, are the third people to live in the island. It was these events of which the Delphic Priestess reminded the Cretans in her answer to their question, and thereby prevented them from joining the Greek confederacy in spite of their readiness to do so.

The Thessalians did not submit to Persia until they were compelled, for they showed plainly enough that the intrigues of the Aleuadae were not to their liking. No sooner had the news reached them of the imminent crossing of the Persian army into Europe than they sent representatives to the Isthmus, where delegates from all Greek towns loyal to the common cause were assembled. On their arrival the Thessalian delegates addressed the assembly in these terms: 'Fellow countrymen, in order to save Thessaly and the whole of Greece, it is necessary to defend the passage past Mt Olympus. We are ready to assist you in the defence of this vital pass, and you, for your part, must send a strong force. If you fail to do so, we give you fair warning that we shall come to terms with Persia. We are in an exposed position, and cannot be expected, alone and unassisted, to give our lives merely to save the rest of you. If you are unwilling to send us aid, you cannot compel us to fight your battle for you; for sheer inability is stronger than any compulsion. We shall try to devise some means of saving ourselves.'

The Greek answer was to determine to send an army by sea to Thessaly, to defend the pass. The troops assembled and, after passing through the Euripus, came to Alus in Achaea, where they left the ships and proceeded to Thessaly on foot. Here they occupied Tempe, the pass which leads from lower Macedonia into Thessaly along the Peneus river, between Mt Olympus and Mt Ossa. It was here that some 10,000 Greek hoplites, reinforced by the Thessalian cavalry, took up their position. The Spartans were commanded by Euanetus son of Carenus, who had been chosen for the post from the Polemarchs, though he was not of the royal blood; the Athenians were commanded by Themistocles, son of Neocles. But the army had not been in Tempe many days when a message arrived from Alexander, the son of Amyntas, in Macedonia advising the Greek troops to withdraw, and not stay in the pass to be trampled underfoot, adding an indication of the strength of the Persian army and fleet. The advice seemed to be sound, and was clearly offered by the Macedonian in a friendly spirit, so the Greeks took it. I think myself that what persuaded them to go was the alarm they felt upon learning that there was another way into Thessaly through upper Macedonia and Perrhaebia, near the town of Gonnus – the pass, in fact, by which Xerxes' army actually did come in.

The Greeks, then, re-embarked and returned to the Isthmus. Such were the circumstances of the expedition to Thessaly – it took place while Xerxes was at Abydos, just before he crossed the strait from Asia into Europe. The result of it was that the Thessalians, finding themselves without support, no longer hesitated but wholeheartedly worked in the Persian interest, so that in the course of the war they proved of the greatest use to Xerxes.

The Greeks on their return to the Isthmus then discussed, in consideration of the warning they had received from Alexander, where they should make a stand. The proposal which found most favour was to guard the pass of Thermopylae, on the grounds that it was narrower than the pass into Thessaly and at the same time nearer home. They knew nothing as yet about the mountain track by means of which the men who fell at Thermopylae were taken in the rear, and only learnt of its existence from the people of Trachis after their arrival.

The decision, then, was to hold the pass in order to prevent the Persians from entering Greece, and at the same time to send the fleet to Artemisium on the coast of Histiaea; for these two places being close together, communication would be easy. The topography is as follows: Artemisium is where the sea south of Thrace contracts into a narrow channel between the island of Sciathus and the mainland of Magnesia; pass through this channel and you come to the strip of coast called Artemisium. It is a part of Euboea, and contains a temple of Artemis. The pass through Trachis into Greece is, at Thermopylae, fifty feet wide; elsewhere, both east and west of Thermopylae, it is still narrower; at Alpeni to the eastward, it is only a single waggon track, and to the westward near Anthela on the river Phoenix it is about the same. To the south-west – inland – there is no way through, passage being barred by a lofty and precipitous ascent, running up to Mt Oeta, while on the other side of the roadway is the sea, full of banks and shoals. There are hot springs in the pass – known locally as the Basins – with an altar over them dedicated to Heracles. A wall was once built across this passage, and there used long ago to be a gateway in it; both were constructed by the Phocians in fear of an invasion from Thessaly, at the period when the Thessalians came from Thesprotia to settle in the country of Aeolis, which they still occupy. The new settlers tried to overrun Phocis, and the Phocians raised the wall as a protective measure, and at the same time turned the water from the hot springs over the pass, to cut up the ground into gullies, resorting to every device to keep the Thessalians out. The wall had been built a very long time ago and most of it had fallen into ruin through age; now, however, it was decided to rebuild it, and to use it to help stop the Persians from getting through into Greece. Quite close to the road is a village called Alpeni, from which the Greeks counted upon drawing supplies.

These, then, were the places which the Greeks thought would best suit their purpose; careful consideration of all the circumstances, and the realization that the Persians would be unable, in the narrow pass, to use their cavalry or take advantage of their numbers, determined them to make their stand at this point against the invader; so when news came that the enemy was in Pieria, they broke up from the Isthmus and proceeded to their new positions, some on foot to Thermopylae, others by sea to Artemisium.

Meanwhile, as the Greek troops hurried to their stations, the people of Delphi, in great alarm for their own safety and for Greece, applied to their oracle for advice. 'Pray to the winds,' was the answer; 'for they will be good allies to Greece.' The first thing the Delphians did upon receiving this oracular counsel was to report it to all the Greek states who were determined to fight for their freedom; and, by thus communicating the divine message at a time when Greece was in the grip of fear at the prospect of invasion, they earned everlasting gratitude. Subsequently they consecrated an altar to the winds at Thyia – a place named after Cephisus' daughter, who has a shrine there – and offered sacrifice upon it to the winds in supplication. In memory of this oracle the Delphians still, to this day, pray to the winds for favour.

Xerxes' fleet now left Therma, and ten of the fastest ships set a course direct for Sciathus, where three Greek vessels, one from Troezen, one from Aegina, and one from Attica, were on the look-out. At the first glimpse of the enemy all three fled. The Persians gave chase; the ship from Troezen, under the command of Prexinus, fell into their hands at once, and her captors, picking out the best-looking of the fighting men on board, took him up forward and cut his throat, thinking, no doubt, that the sacrifice of their first handsome Greek prisoner would benefit their cause. The man's name was Leon – and possibly his name had something to do with his fate. The trireme from Aegina, commanded by Asonides, gave the Persians some trouble. One of the soldiers on board – Pytheas, the son of Ischenous – distinguished himself that day; for after the ship was taken, he continued to resist until he was nearly cut to pieces. At last he fell, but, as there was still breath in his body, the Persian troops, anxious to do all they could to save the life of so brave a man, dressed his wounds with myrrh and bound them up with linen bandages. On returning to their base, they exhibited their prisoner admiringly to everybody there, and treated him with much kindness. The other prisoners from this ship they treated merely as slaves.

Two of the three Greek vessels thus fell into Persian hands; the third, commanded by the Athenian Phormus, went ashore, while trying to escape, at the mouth of the Peneus. Here she was taken, though the men in her got away; for the instant the vessel grounded the Athenians aboard leapt out and made their way back to Athens through Thessaly.

News of what had happened was flashed to the Greeks at Artemisium by fire-signal from Sciathus. In the panic which ensued they left their station and moved to Chalcis, intending to guard the Euripus, and leaving look-outs on the high ground of Euboea. Three of the ten Persian ships ran aground on the Ant, a sunken reef between Sciathus and Magnesia; in consequence of this the Persians marked the reef with a stone beacon, after which, the danger being removed, the whole fleet set sail from Therma, eleven days after Xerxes had marched from the town with his army. The Ant lies right in the fairway; Pammon, a native of Scyros, took the Persians to it when they erected their beacon. A day's voyage brought the Persian fleet to Sepias in Magnesia and the strip of coast between Cape Sepias and the town of Casthanea.

The Persian fleet got as far as Sepias, and the army as far as Thermopylae, without loss. I find by calculation that their numbers up to this stage were as follows: first there was the fleet of 1207 ships belonging to the various nations which sailed from Asia, with its original complement of 241,400 men – allowing 200 to each ship. Each of these vessels carried, apart from native soldiers – or marines – and in addition to the crew, thirty fighting men who were either Persians, Medes, or Sacae, making an additional 36,210. Add to these the crews of the penteconters, carrying roughly 80 men apiece; there were, as I have already said, 3000 penteconters, so this will make another 240,000. This was the naval force brought by Xerxes from Asia, and the total number of men aboard comes to 517,610.

As to the army, the infantry was 1,700,000 strong and the cavalry 80,000. Then there were the Arabian camel corps and the Libyan charioteers, which I reckon as a further 20,000. The grand total, therefore, of land and sea forces brought over from Asia was 2,317,610, excluding army servants and the men in the food transports.

To this, moreover, must be added the troops which were collected as Xerxes passed through Europe. Here I must be content with a rough estimate. The Greeks of Thrace and of the islands off the coast furnished, I should say, 120 ships: this would make 24,000 men. The strength of the infantry furnished by the Thracians, Paeonians, Eordi, Bottiaei, Chalcidians, Brygi, Pierians, Macedonians, Perrhaebians, Enionians, Dolopes, Magnetes, Achaeans, and the coastal settlements of Thrace, I would put at 300,000. So by adding these to the original force from Asia we get a total of 2,641,610 fighting men. Lastly, it is my belief that the army servants and camp followers, the crews of the provision boats and of other craft which sailed with the expedition were not less, but more, numerous than the actual fighting troops; however I will reckon them as neither more nor fewer, but as equal, and thus arrive at my final estimate, which is, that Xerxes, the son of Darius, reached Sepias and Thermopylae at the head of an army consisting, in all, of 5,283,220 men.

So much for the actual army and its attendants; as for eunuchs, female cooks, and concubines, no one could attempt an estimate of their number, any more than of the various pack-animals and Indian dogs which followed the army. They were far too numerous to count. I am not surprised that with so many people and so many beasts the rivers sometimes failed to provide enough water; what does amaze me is that the food never gave out, for I reckon that if no more than a quart of meal was the daily ration for one man, the total daily consumption would have amounted to 110,340 bushels – and this without counting what was consumed by the women, eunuchs, pack-animals, and dogs. Amongst all these immense numbers there was not a man who, for stature and noble bearing, was more worthy than Xerxes to wield so vast a power.

The Persian fleet, as I have mentioned, made the Magnesian coast between the town of Casthanea and Cape Sepias, and on its arrival the leading ships made fast to the land, while the remainder, as there was not much room on the short stretch of beach, came to anchor and lay offshore in lines, eight deep. In this position they remained during the night; but at dawn next day the weather, which was clear and calm, suddenly changed, and the fleet was caught in a heavy blow from the east – a 'Hellespontian', as the people there call it – which raised a confused sea like a pot on the boil. Those who realized in time that the blow was coming, and all who happened to be lying in a convenient position, managed to beach their vessels and to get them clear of the water before they were damaged, and thus saved their own lives as well; but the ships which were caught offshore were driven, some on to the place called the Ovens at the foot of Mt Pelion, others on to the beach itself; a number were driven on to Sepias, and others, again, were forced ashore off the towns of Meliboea and Casthanea. The storm was very violent and there was no chance of riding it out.

There is a story that the Athenians had called upon Boreas to help them, in consequence of another oracle, by which they were advised to 'ask the assistance of their son-in-law'. Boreas, according to the Greek account, married a woman of Attica, Erechtheus' daughter

Orithyia, and in consequence of this marriage the Athenians (so the tale goes) supposed Boreas to be their son-in-law; so when they observed from their station at Chalcis in Euboea that a storm was coming – or possibly even sooner – they offered sacrifice to Boreas and Orithyia and begged them to come to their aid and to repeat the former disaster at Athos by once again destroying the Persian fleet. I cannot say if this was really the reason why the fleet was caught at anchor by the north-easter, but the Athenians are quite positive about it: Boreas, they maintain, had helped them before, and it was Boreas who was responsible for what occurred on this occasion too. On their return home they built him a shrine by the river Ilissus.

Four hundred ships, at the lowest estimate, are said to have been lost in this disaster, and the loss of life and of treasure was beyond reckoning. It proved, however, to be a very good thing indeed for a certain Magnesian named Ameinocles, the son of Cretines, who owned land in the neighbourhood of Sepias; for he subsequently picked up a large number of gold and silver drinking-cups which were washed ashore, and found Persian treasure-chests containing more gold, beyond counting. This made him a very rich man, though in other respects he proved less fortunate; for he met with the distressing disaster of having killed his son.

The number of merchant vessels and other craft lost in the storm was too great to reckon. Indeed, such was the magnitude of the disaster that the Persian naval commanders, fearing that the Thessalians might take advantage of their desperate plight to attack them, protected themselves by building a high barricade out of the wreckage. The storm lasted three days, after which the Magi brought it to an end by sacrificial offerings, and by putting spells on the wind, and by further offerings to Thetis and the sea-nymphs – or, of course, it may be that the wind just dropped naturally. The reason why the Magi sacrificed to Thetis was that they had learnt from the Ionians that she was supposed to have been carried off from here by Peleus, and that all the headland of Sepias was sacred to her and the other daughters of Nereus. In any case, on the fourth day the weather was fine again.

On the second day of the storm the look-out men on the Euboean hills came hurrying to the Greeks and described in detail the destruction of the Persian ships. On hearing the news, they offered prayers of thanks-giving and libations of wine to Poseidon the saviour, and made all speed to return to their station at Artemisium, in the expectation that only a few ships would be left to oppose them. For the second time, therefore, they lay off Artemisium. From that day to this they have always addressed Poseidon by the title of Saviour.

Meanwhile, after the wind had dropped and the sea had gone down, the Persians got the ships they had hauled ashore into the water again, and proceeded along the coast round the southern point of Magnesia straight into the bay which leads to Pagasae. There is a place in this bay where it is said that Heracles, at the start of the voyage of the *Argo* to fetch the Golden Fleece from Aea in Colchis, was put ashore by Jason and his companions to get water, and was left behind. The place got the name of Aphetae – 'putting forth' – because it was the intention of the Argonauts to make it their point of departure after watering the ship. It was here that Xerxes' fleet brought up.

Fifteen of the Persian ships were far behind in getting under way, and the men aboard, happening to catch sight of the Greek ships at Artemisium, mistook them for their own, and on making towards them fell into the enemies' hands. These vessels were under the command of Sandoces, the son of Thamasius and governor of Cyme in Aeolis. Sandoces, who was one of the royal judges, had been arrested by Darius some time before and crucified, on a charge of perverting justice for money. But while he was actually on the cross, Darius came to the conclusion that his services to the royal house outweighed his offences, and realizing in consequence that he had acted with more promptitude than wisdom, caused him to be taken down. Thus he escaped with his life from King Darius, but this time, when he fell foul of the Greek navy, he was not destined to escape again; for as soon as the Greeks saw his squadron approaching they realized his mistake, put to sea, and captured it without difficulty. Amongst the prisoners in one of the ships was Aridolis, the tyrant of Alabanda in Caria; in another was Penthylus, the son of Demonous, the Paphian commander, who had brought twelve ships from Paphos. Eleven of them were lost at Sepias in the storm, and he was taken as he sailed to Artemisium in the only one which survived. The Greeks questioned these two prisoners on all they wished to know about

Xerxes' forces, and then sent them away in chains to the Isthmus of Corinth.

Meanwhile the Persian fleet, with the exception of the fifteen ships under Sandoces' command, arrived safely at Aphetae. Two days previously Xerxes with the army had passed through Thessaly and Achaea and entered the country of the Malians. While he was in Thessaly he had held races between the native horses and his own, because he had heard that the horses of Thessaly were the best in Greece. The Greek mares were, however, soundly beaten. Of the Thessalian rivers, the only one which failed to supply enough water for the troops was the Onochonus; but in Achaea even the biggest – the Apidanus – scarcely sufficed.

At Halos in Achaea Xerxes' guides, wishing to give him all the information they could, told him the local account about the Laphystian Zeus. The story is that Athamas, the son of Aeolus, plotted with Ino the death of Phrixus; subsequently the Achaeans in obedience to an oracle laid a penalty upon the descendants of Phrixus and his son Cytissorus: this was that the eldest of the family should be forbidden to enter the Council Chamber – or People's House, as the Achaeans call it – and that they themselves should keep watch to see that the ban was observed. If one of them does enter the Chamber, he can never get out again except to be offered as a sacrifice. They went on to relate that many of them, when recognized entering the Chamber and threatened with death in this way, escape in terror to some other country, and perhaps return long afterwards. They further described to Xerxes the ritual of the sacrifice, how the man was always made to wear a wreath, and was led to his death in a solemn procession. The reason why the descendants of Cytissorus and Phrixus are forced to endure this treatment is that when the Achaeans were about to kill Aeolus' son Athamas as a sin-offering, or scapegoat, on behalf of their country, Cytissorus came from Aea in Colchis and rescued him, thus calling down the wrath of God upon his descendants.

In consequence of this story Xerxes kept clear of the sacred ground and issued orders to his army to do the same; he showed respect also to the house and precinct of the family of Athamas.

From Thessaly and Achaea Xerxes went on into Malis, following the coast of a bay in which there is a daily rise and fall of tide. The country round this bay is flat – broad in one part, very narrow in another; all round is a chain of lofty and trackless mountains, called the Cliffs of Trachis, which enclose the whole territory of Malis. As one comes from Achaea, the first town on the bay is Anticyra, near to which is the mouth of the Spercheius, a river which comes down from the country of the Enianes. Some three and a half miles further on there is another river, the Dyras, which, according to the legend, burst from the ground to help Heracles when he was burning; then, at about the same distance, is a third stream, the Melas, and rather more than half a mile beyond that is the town of Trachis. At Trachis the space between the hills and the sea is more extensive than anywhere else, the area of the plain being over 5000 acres. South of Trachis there is a cleft in the ring of hills;

through it the river Asopus issues, and comes down to the foot of the hills. Further south another small stream, the Phoenix, runs down from the hills and joins the Asopus. It is at the Phoenix that the plain is narrowest, there being room here only for a single cart-track. From the Phoenix to Thermopylae is about two miles, and between them lies the village of Anthela, which the Asopus passes just before it reaches the sea. Round Anthela the ground is more open; there is a temple there dedicated to Demeter of the Amphictyons, as well as seats for the deputies of the Amphictyonic league, and a shrine of Amphictyon himself.

The position, then, was that Xerxes was lying with his force at Trachis in Malian territory, while the Greeks occupied the pass known locally as Pylae – though Thermopylae is the common Greek name. Such were the respective positions of the two armies, one being in control of all the country from Trachis northward, the other of the whole mainland to the south. The Greek force which here awaited the coming of Xerxes was made up of the following contingents: 300 hoplites from Sparta, 500 from Tegea, 500 from Mantinea, 120 from Orchomenus in Arcadia, 1000 from the rest of Arcadia; from Corinth there were 400, from Phlius 200, and from Mycenae 80. In addition to these troops from the Peloponnese, there were the Boeotian contingents of 700 from Thespiae and 400 from Thebes. The Locrians of Opus and the Phocians had also obeyed the call to arms, the former sending all the men they had, the latter one thousand. The other Greeks had induced these two towns to send troops by a message to the effect that they themselves were merely an advance force, and that the main body of the allies was daily expected; the sea, moreover, was strongly held by the fleet of Athens and Aegina and the other naval forces. Thus there was no cause for alarm – for, after all, it was not a god who threatened Greece, but a man, and there neither was nor ever would be a man who was not born with a good chance of misfortune – and the greater the man, the greater the misfortune. The present enemy was no exception; he too was human, and was sure to be disappointed of his great expectations.

The appeal succeeded, and Opus and Phocis sent their troops to Trachis. The contingents of the various states were under their own officers, but the most respected was Leonidas the Spartan, who was in command of the whole army. Leonidas traced his descent directly back to Heracles, through Anaxandrides and Leon (his father and grandfather), Eurycratides, Anaxander, Eurycrates, Polydorus, Alcamenes, Telechles, Archelaus, Agesilaus, Doryssus, Leobotas, Echestratus, Agis, Eurysthenes, Aristodemus, Aristomachus, Cleodaeus – and so to Hyllus, who was Heracles' son. He had come to be king of Sparta quite unexpectedly, for as he had two elder brothers, Cleomenes and Dorieus, he had no thought of himself succeeding to the throne. Dorieus, however, was killed in Sicily, and when Cleomenes also died without an heir, Leonidas found himself next in the succession. He was older than Cleombrotus, Anaxandrides' youngest son, and was, moreover, married to Cleomenes' daughter. The three hundred men whom he brought on this occasion to Thermopylae were chosen by himself, all

fathers of living sons. He also took with him the Thebans
I mentioned, under the command of Leontiades, the son
of Eurymachus. The reason why he made a special point
of taking troops from Thebes, and from Thebes only,
was that the Thebans were strongly suspected of Persian
sympathies, so he called upon them to play their part in
the war in order to see if they would answer the call, or
openly refuse to join the confederacy. They did send
troops, but their sympathy was nevertheless with the
enemy. Leonidas and his three hundred were sent by
Sparta in advance of the main army, in order that the
sight of them might encourage the other confederates
to fight and prevent them from going over to the enemy,
as they were quite capable of doing if they knew that
Sparta was hanging back; the intention was, when the
Carneia was over (for it was that festival which prevented
the Spartans from taking the field in the ordinary way),
to leave a garrison in the city and march with all the
troops at their disposal. The other allied states proposed
to act similarly; for the Olympic festival happened to fall
just at this same period. None of them ever expected the
battle at Thermopylae to be decided so soon – which
was the reason why they sent only advance parties there.

The Persian army was now close to the pass, and the
Greeks, suddenly doubting their power to resist, held a
conference to consider the advisability of retreat. It was
proposed by the Peloponnesians generally that the army
should fall back upon the Peloponnese and hold the
Isthmus; but when the Phocians and Locrians expressed
their indignation at this suggestion, Leonidas gave his
vote for staying where they were and sending, at the

same time, an appeal for reinforcements to the various states of the confederacy, as their numbers were inadequate to cope with the Persians.

During the conference Xerxes sent a man on horseback to ascertain the strength of the Greek force and to observe what the troops were doing. He had heard before he left Thessaly that a small force was concentrated here, led by the Lacedaemonians under Leonidas of the house of Heracles. The Persian rider approached the camp and took a thorough survey of all he could see – which was not, however, the whole Greek army; for the men on the further side of the wall which, after its reconstruction, was now guarded, were out of sight. He did, none the less, carefully observe the troops who were stationed on the outside of the wall. At that moment these happened to be the Spartans, and some of them were stripped for exercise, while others were combing their hair. The Persian spy watched them in astonishment; nevertheless he made sure of their numbers, and of everything else he needed to know, as accurately as he could, and then rode quietly off. No one attempted to catch him, or took the least notice of him.

Back in his own camp he told Xerxes what he had seen. Xerxes was bewildered; the truth, namely that the Spartans were preparing themselves to die and deal death with all their strength, was beyond his comprehension, and what they were doing seemed to him merely absurd. Accordingly he sent for Demaratus, the son of Ariston, who had come with the army, and questioned him about the spy's report, in the hope of finding out what the behaviour of the Spartans might mean. 'Once before,'

Demaratus said, 'when we began our march against Greece, you heard me speak of these men. I told you then how I saw this enterprise would turn out, and you laughed at me. I strive for nothing, my lord, more earnestly than to observe the truth in your presence; so hear me once more. These men have come to fight us for possession of the pass, and for that struggle they are preparing. It is the custom of the Spartans to pay careful attention to their hair when they are about to risk their lives. But I assure you that if you can defeat these men and the rest of the Spartans who are still at home, there is no other people in the world who will dare to stand firm or lift a hand against you. You have now to deal with the finest kingdom in Greece, and with the bravest men.'

Xerxes, unable to believe what Demaratus said, asked further how it was possible that so small a force could fight with his army. 'My lord,' Demaratus replied, 'treat me as a liar, if what I have foretold does not take place.' But still Xerxes was unconvinced.

For four days Xerxes waited, in constant expectation that the Greeks would make good their escape; then, on the fifth, when still they had made no move and their continued presence seemed mere impudent and reckless folly, he was seized with rage and sent forward the Medes and Cissians with orders to take them alive and bring them into his presence. The Medes charged, and in the struggle which ensued many fell; but others took their places, and in spite of terrible losses refused to be beaten off. They made it plain enough to anyone, and not least to the king himself, that he had in his army many men, indeed, but few soldiers. All day the battle continued; the Medes, after their rough handling, were at length withdrawn and their place was taken by Hydarnes and his picked Persian troops – the King's Immortals – who advanced to the attack in full confidence of bringing the business to a quick and easy end. But, once engaged, they were no more successful than the Medes had been; all went as before, the two armies fighting in a confined space, the Persians using shorter spears than the Greeks and having no advantage from their numbers.

On the Spartan side it was a memorable fight; they were men who understood war pitted against an inexperienced enemy, and amongst the feints they employed was to turn their backs in a body and pretend to be retreating in confusion, whereupon the enemy would pursue them with a great clatter and roar; but the Spartans, just as the Persians were on them, would wheel and face them and inflict in the new struggle innumerable casualties. The Spartans had their losses too, but not many. At last the Persians, finding that their assaults upon the pass, whether by divisions or by any other way they could think of, were all useless, broke off the engagement and withdrew. Xerxes was watching the battle from where he sat; and it is said that in the course of the attacks three times, in terror for his army, he leapt to his feet.

Next day the fighting began again, but with no better success for the Persians, who renewed their onslaught in the hope that the Greeks, being so few in number, might be badly enough disabled by wounds to prevent further resistance. But the Greeks never slackened; their troops were ordered in divisions corresponding to the states from which they came, and each division took its turn in the line except the Phocian, which had been posted to guard the track over the mountains. So when the Persians found that things were no better for them than on the previous day, they once more withdrew.

How to deal with the situation Xerxes had no idea; but just then, a man from Malis, Ephialtes, the son of Eurydemus, came, in hope of a rich reward, to tell the king about the track which led over the hills to Thermopylae – and thus he was to prove the death of the Greeks who held the pass.

Later on, Ephialtes, in fear of the Spartans, fled to Thessaly, and in his absence a price was put upon his head by the Amphictyons assembled at Pylae. Some time afterwards he returned to Anticyra, where he was killed by Athenades of Trachis. Athenades killed him not for his treachery but for another reason, which I will explain further on; but the Spartans honoured him none the less on that account. According to another story, it was Onetes, the son of Phanagoras of Carystus, and Corydallus of Anticyra who spoke to Xerxes and showed the Persians the way round by the mountain track. This is entirely unconvincing, my first criterion being the fact that the Amphictyons, presumably after careful inquiry, set a price not upon Onetes and Corydallus but upon Ephialtes of Trachis, and my second, that there is no doubt that the accusation of treachery was the reason for Ephialtes' flight. Certainly Onetes, even though he was not a native of Malis, might have known about the track, if he had spent much time in the neighbourhood

– but it was Ephialtes, and no one else, who showed the Persians the way, and I put his name on record as the guilty one.

Xerxes found Ephialtes' offer most satisfactory. He was delighted with it, and promptly sent off Hydarnes with the troops under his command. They left camp about the time the lamps are lit.

The track was originally discovered by the Malians of the neighbourhood; they afterwards used it to help the Thessalians, taking them over it to attack Phocis at the time when the Phocians were protected from invasion by the wall which they had built across the pass. So long, then, have its sinister uses been known to the Malians! The track begins at the Asopus, the stream which flows through the narrow gorge, and, running along the ridge of the mountain – which, like the track itself, is called Anopaea – ends at Alpenos, the first Locrian settlement as one comes from Malis, near the rock known as Black-Buttocks' Stone and the seats of the Cercopes. Just here is the narrowest part of the pass.

This, then, was the mountain track which the Persians took, after crossing the Asopus. They marched throughout the night, with the mountains of Oeta on their right hand and those of Trachis on their left. By early dawn they were at the summit of the ridge, near the spot where the Phocians, as I mentioned before, stood on guard with a thousand men, to watch the track and protect their country. The Phocians had volunteered for this service to Leonidas, the lower road being held as already described.

The ascent of the Persians had been concealed by the

oak-woods which cover all these hills, and it was only when they were up that the Phocians became aware of their approach; for there was no wind, and the marching feet made a loud swishing and rustling in the fallen leaves. Leaping to their feet, the Phocians were in the act of arming themselves when the enemy was upon them. The Persians were surprised at the sight of troops preparing to resist; they had expected no opposition – yet here was a body of men barring their way. Hydarnes asked Ephialtes who they were, for his first fearful thought was that they might be Spartans; but on learning the truth he prepared to engage them. The Persian arrows flew thick and fast, and the Phocians, supposing themselves to be the main object of the attack, hurriedly withdrew to the highest point of the mountain, where they made ready to face destruction. But the Persians with Ephialtes and Hydarnes paid no further attention to them, but passed on along the descending track with all possible speed.

The Greeks at Thermopylae had their first warning of the death that was coming with the dawn from the seer Megistias, who read their doom in the victims of sacrifice; deserters, too, came in during the night with news of the Persian flank movement, and lastly, just as day was breaking, the look-out men came running from the hills. In council of war their opinions were divided, some urging that they must not abandon their post, others the opposite. The result was that the army split: some dispersed, contingents returning to their various cities, while others made ready to stand by Leonidas. It is said that Leonidas himself dismissed them, to spare their lives, but thought it unbecoming for the Spartans under his command to desert the post which they had originally come to guard. I myself am inclined to think that he dismissed them when he realized that they had no heart for the fight and were unwilling to take their share of the danger; at the same time honour forbade that he himself should go. And indeed by remaining at his post he left great glory behind him, and Sparta did not lose her prosperity, as might otherwise have happened; for right at the outset of the war the Spartans had been told by the Delphic oracle that either their city must be laid waste by the foreigner or a Spartan king be killed. The prophecy was in hexameter verse and ran as follows:

Hear your fate, O dwellers in Sparta of the wide spaces;
Either your famed, great town must be sacked by Perseus'
   sons,
Or, if that be not, the whole land of Lacedaemon
Shall mourn the death of a king of the house of Heracles,
For not the strength of lions or of bulls shall hold him,
Strength against strength; for he has the power of Zeus,
And will not be checked till one of these two he has
   consumed.

I believe it was the thought of this oracle, combined with his wish to lay up for the Spartans a treasure of fame in which no other city should share, that made Leonidas dismiss those troops; I do not think that they deserted, or went off without orders, because of a difference of opinion. Moreover, I am strongly supported in this view by the case of the seer Megistias, who was with the army

– an Acarnanian, said to be of the clan of Melampus – who foretold the coming doom from his inspection of the sacrificial victims. He quite plainly received orders from Leonidas to quit Thermopylae, to save him from sharing the army's fate. He refused to go, but he sent his only son, who was serving with the forces.

Thus it was that the confederate troops, by Leonidas' orders, abandoned their posts and left the pass, all except the Thespians and the Thebans who remained with the Spartans. The Thebans were detained by Leonidas as hostages very much against their will; but the Thespians of their own accord refused to desert Leonidas and his men, and stayed, and died with them. They were under the command of Demophilus the son of Diadromes.

In the morning Xerxes poured a libation to the rising sun, and then waited until the time when the market-place is filled before he began to move forward. This was according to Ephialtes' instructions, for the way down from the ridge is much shorter and more direct than the long and circuitous ascent. As the Persian army advanced to the assault, the Greeks under Leonidas, knowing that they were going to their deaths, went out into the wider part of the pass much further than they had done before; in the previous days' fighting they had been holding the wall and making sorties from behind it into the narrow neck, but now they fought outside the narrows. Many of the barbarians fell; behind them the company commanders plied their whips indiscriminately, driving the men on. Many fell into the sea and were drowned, and still more were trampled to death by one another. No one could count the number of the dead. The Greeks, who knew that the enemy were on their way round by the mountain track and that death was inevitable, put forth all their strength and fought with fury and desperation. By this time most of their spears were broken, and they were killing Persians with their swords.

In the course of that fight Leonidas fell, having fought most gallantly, and many distinguished Spartans with him – their names I have learned, as those of men who deserve to be remembered; indeed, I have learned the names of all the three hundred. Amongst the Persian dead, too, were many men of high distinction, including two brothers of Xerxes, Habrocomes and Hyperanthes, sons of Darius by Artanes' daughter Phratagune. Artanes, the son of Hystaspes and grandson of Arsames, was Darius' brother; as Phratagune was his only child, his giving her to Darius was equivalent to giving him his entire estate.

There was a bitter struggle over the body of Leonidas; four times the Greeks drove the enemy off, and at last by their valour rescued it. So it went on, until the troops with Ephialtes were close at hand; and then, when the Greeks knew that they had come, the character of the fighting changed. They withdrew again into the narrow neck of the pass, behind the wall, and took up a position in a single compact body – all except the Thebans – on the little hill at the entrance to the pass, where the stone lion in memory of Leonidas stands today. Here they resisted to the last, with their swords, if they had them, and, if not, with their hands and teeth, until the Persians, coming on from the front over the ruins of the wall and closing in from behind, finally overwhelmed them with missile weapons.

Of all the Spartans and Thespians who fought so valiantly the most signal proof of courage was given by the Spartan Dieneces. It is said that before the battle he was told by a native of Trachis that, when the Persians shot their arrows, there were so many of them that they hid the sun. Dieneces, however, quite unmoved by the thought of the strength of the Persian army, merely remarked: 'This is pleasant news that the stranger from Trachis brings us: if the Persians hide the sun, we shall have our battle in the shade.' He is said to have left on record other sayings, too, of a similar kind, by which he will be remembered. After Dieneces the greatest distinction was won by two Spartan brothers, Alpheus and Maron, the sons of Orsiphantus; and of the Thespians the man to gain the highest glory was a certain Dithyrambus, the son of Harmatides.

The dead were buried where they fell, and with them the men who had been killed before those dismissed by Leonidas left the pass. Over them is this inscription, in honour of the whole force:

> Four thousand here from Pelops' land
> Against three million once did stand.

The Spartans have a special epitaph; it runs:

> Go tell the Spartans, you who read:
> We took their orders, and here lie dead.

For the seer Megistias there is the following:

> Here lies Megistias, who died
> When the Mede passed Spercheius' tide.
> A prophet; yet he scorned to save
> Himself, but shared the Spartans' grave.

The columns with the epitaphs inscribed on them were erected in honour of the dead by the Amphictyons – though the epitaph upon the seer Megistias was the work of Simonides, the son of Leoprepes, who put it there for friendship's sake.

Two of the three hundred Spartans, Eurytus and Aristodemus, are said to have been suffering from acute inflammation of the eyes, on account of which they were dismissed by Leonidas before the battle and went to Alpeni to recuperate. These two men might have agreed together to return in safety to Sparta; or, if they did not wish to do so, they might have shared the fate of their friends. But, unable to agree which course to take, they quarrelled, and Eurytus had no sooner heard that the Persians had made their way round by the mountain track than he called for his armour, put it on, and ordered his helot to lead him to the scene of the battle. The helot obeyed, and then took to his heels, and Eurytus, plunging into the thick of things, was killed. Aristodemus, on the other hand, finding that his heart failed him, stayed behind at Alpeni. Now if only Aristodemus had been involved – if he alone had returned sick to Sparta – or if they had both gone back together, I do not think that the Spartans would have been angry; but as one was killed and the other took advantage of the excuse, which was open to both of them, to save his skin, they could hardly help being very angry indeed with Aristodemus.

There is another explanation of how Aristodemus got back alive to Sparta: according to this, he was sent from camp with a message, and though he might have returned in time to take part in the fighting, he deliberately loitered on the way and so saved himself, while the man who accompanied him on the errand joined in the battle and was killed. In any case, he was met upon his return with reproach and disgrace; no Spartan would give him a light to kindle his fire, or speak to him, and he was called a Trembler. However, he afterwards made amends for everything at the battle of Plataea.

There is also a story that one more of the three hundred – Pantites – survived. He had been sent with a message into Thessaly, and on his return to Sparta found himself in such disgrace that he hanged himself.

The Thebans under Leontiades remained for a time with the army and were compelled to make some show of resistance to the enemy; but as soon as they saw that things were going in favour of Persia, they took the opportunity of Leonidas' hurried retreat to the little hill, where his last stand was made, to detach themselves from his force; they then approached the enemy with outstretched hands, crying out that in their zeal for the Persian interest they had been amongst the first to give earth and water to the king, and had no share in the responsibility for the injury done him, because they had come to Thermopylae against their will. And when it was backed up by the evidence of the Thessalians, it saved their lives. Nevertheless, their luck did not hold in every respect; for a few were killed by the Persians on their first approach, and all the rest were branded by Xerxes' orders with the royal mark, beginning with Leontiades their commander. Leontiades' son Eurymachus was afterwards killed by the Plataeans when he was leading a force of four hundred Theban troops at the capture of Plataea.

Such, then, is the story of the Greeks' struggle at Thermopylae. Xerxes, when the battle was over, summoned Demaratus to ask him some questions. 'Demaratus,' he began, 'you are a good man – the truth of your words proves it. Everything has turned out as you said it would. Now tell me – how many more Lacedaemonians are there? And how many of them are as good soldiers as these were? Or are they all as good?' 'Sire,' Demaratus answered, 'there are a great many men and many towns in Lacedaemon; but what you really want to know I will now tell you: there is in that country a town called Sparta, which contains about eight thousand men. All these are the equals of those who fought in this battle. The other men in Lacedaemon are not their equals – but good soldiers none the less.'

'Demaratus,' said Xerxes, 'tell me what you think would be the easiest way of defeating these people. You were once their king, so you must be well acquainted with all the ins and outs of their policy.'

'Sire,' replied Demaratus, 'if you are really serious in asking my advice, I am bound to tell you what I consider the best plan. Suppose you send three hundred ships from the fleet to Lacedaemon. Off the coast there is an island called Cythera – Chilon, the wisest man who ever lived amongst us, once said that it would be better for the Spartans if it were sunk beneath the sea, for he always expected that it would provide just such an opportunity for a hostile force as what I am now suggesting. It was not, of course, your attack that he foresaw – it was the prospect of any attack from any quarter that alarmed him. This, then, is my proposal: let your ships make Cythera their base, and from it spread terror over Lacedaemon. With a war of their own, on their own doorstep, as it were, you need not fear that they will help the other Greeks while your army is engaged in conquering them. Thus the rest of Greece will be enslaved first and Lacedaemon will be left alone and helpless. On the other hand, if you decide against this plan, you may expect more trouble; for there is a narrow isthmus in the Peloponnese, and in it you will find all the troops from that part of Greece who have formed a league to resist you, and you will have to face bloodier battles than any you have yet witnessed. But if you take my advice, the Isthmus and the Peloponnesian towns will fall into your hands without a blow.'

Achaemenes, Xerxes' brother and commander of the fleet, who happened to be present and was afraid Xerxes might be persuaded to adopt Demaratus' proposal, spoke in answer; 'My lord,' he said, 'I see that you are allowing yourself to be influenced by a man who envies your success, and is probably a traitor to you. He is a typical Greek, and this is just how they love to behave – envying anyone else's good fortune and hating any power greater than their own. In our present circumstances, when we have already had four hundred ships wrecked, if you detach another three hundred from the fleet for a voyage round the Peloponnese, the enemy will be a match for us. Keep the fleet together, and they will never dare risk an engagement – the disparity in numbers will see to that; moreover, if fleet and army keep in touch and advance together, each can support the other; separate them, and you will be no more use to the fleet than the fleet to you. Only lay your own plans soundly, and you can afford not to worry about the enemy, or to keep wondering what they will do, how many they are, or where they will elect to make a stand. They are quite capable of managing their own affairs, just as we are of managing ours. If the Spartans risk another battle with us, they will certainly not repair the injury they have already received.'

'Achaemenes,' Xerxes replied, 'I think you are right, and I will take your advice. Nevertheless, though Demaratus' judgement is not so good as yours, he told me in good faith what he thought best for me. I will not accept your suggestion that he is secretly hostile to my cause; I have evidence of his loyalty in what he has said on previous occasions, and, apart from that, there is the well-known fact that a man often hates his next-door neighbour and is jealous of his success, and when asked for advice will not tell him what he really thinks will help him most – unless, indeed, he is a man of exceptional virtue, such as one seldom finds. But the relationship between men of different countries is very different from that between men of the same town; a man is full of sympathy for the good fortune of a foreign friend, and will always give him the best advice he can. Demaratus is a foreigner and my guest; I should be obliged, therefore, if everyone would refrain from maligning him in future.'

After this conversation Xerxes went over the battle-field to see the bodies, and having been told that Leonidas was king of Sparta and commander of the Spartan force, ordered his head to be cut off and fixed on a stake. This is in my opinion the strongest evidence – though there is plenty more – that King Xerxes, while Leonidas was still alive, felt fiercer anger against him than against any other man; had that not been so, he would never have committed this outrage upon his body; for normally the Persians, more than any other nation I know of, honour men who distinguish themselves in war. However, Xerxes' order was carried out.

I will now return to a point in my story where I omitted to mention something. The Spartans were the first to get the news that Xerxcs was preparing an expedition against Greece; thereupon they sent to the Delphic oracle and received the answer of which I spoke a little while ago. The way they received the news was very remarkable: Demaratus, the son of Ariston, who was an exile in Persia, was not, I imagine – and as is only natural to suppose – well disposed towards the Spartans; so it is open to question whether what he did was inspired by benevolence or by malicious pleasure. Anyway, as soon as news reached him at Susa that Xerxes had decided upon the invasion of Greece, he felt that he must pass on the information to Sparta. As the danger of discovery was great, there was only one way in which he could contrive to get the message through: this was by scraping the wax off a pair of wooden folding tablets, writing on the wood underneath what Xerxes intended to do, and then covering the message over with wax again. In this way the tablets, being apparently blank, would cause no trouble with the guards along the road. When the message reached its destination, no one was able to guess the secret until, as I understand, Cleomenes' daughter Gorgo, who was the wife of Leonidas, divined it and told the others that, if they scraped the wax off, they would find something written on the wood underneath. This was done; the message was revealed and read, and afterwards passed on to the other Greeks. That, at any rate, is the story of what happened.

The following is the roll of the Greek naval force: 127 ships from Athens – partly manned by the Plataeans, whose courage and patriotism led them to undertake this service in spite of their ignorance of nautical matters; 40 from Corinth, 20 from Megara, 20 more from Athens manned by crews from Chalcis, 18 from Aegina, 12 from Sicyon, 10 from Sparta, 8 from Epidaurus, 7 from Eretria, 5 from Troezen, 2 from Styra, and 2 – together with two penteconters – from Ceos. Lastly, the Locrians of Opus joined with seven penteconters.

These, then, were the states which sent ships to Artemisium, and I have given the number which each contributed. The total strength of the fleet, excluding the penteconters, was thus 271 ships of war. The general officer in command, Eurybiades, the son of Eurycleides, was provided by Sparta; for the other members of the confederacy had stipulated for a Lacedaemonian commander, declaring that rather than serve under an Athenian they would break up the intended expedition altogether. From the first, even before Sicily was asked to join the alliance, there had been talk of the advisability of giving Athens command of the fleet; but the proposal had not been well received by the allied states, and the Athenians waived their claim in the interest of national survival, knowing that a quarrel about the command would certainly mean the destruction of Greece. They were, indeed, perfectly right; for the evil of internal strife is worse than united war in the same proportion as war itself is worse than peace. It was their realization of the danger attendant upon lack of unity which made them waive their claim, and they continued to do so as long as Greece desperately needed their help. This was made plain enough by their subsequent action; for when the Persians had been driven from Greece and the war had been carried to Persian territory, the Athenians made the insufferable behaviour of Pausanias their excuse for depriving the Lacedaemonians of the command.

When the Greeks on their arrival at Artemisium found a large Persian fleet lying at Aphetae and all the neighbourhood full of troops, it was evident to them that things had gone very differently with the Persians from what they had expected. They were seized by panic, and began to consider abandoning Artemisium and making their escape into the inner parts of Greece. This greatly alarmed the Euboeans, who no sooner realized what they had in mind than they begged Eurybiades to stay at any rate long enough to allow them to move their children and servants to a place of safety. Eurybiades refused, whereupon they went to Themistocles, the Athenian commander, and by a bribe of thirty talents induced him so to arrange matters that the Greek fleet should stay and fight on the coast of Euboea. The method Themistocles adopted to attain this object was to pass on to Eurybiades, as if it were a personal present from himself, a sixth part of the sum he had received from the Euboeans. This was enough to secure Eurybiades' consent; of the other commanders, however, there was still one who hesitated – Adeimantus son of Ocytus, the Corinthian, who declared that he would withdraw his ships from Artemisium. To him, therefore, Themistocles now addressed himself. 'Never,' he cried with an oath, 'shall you leave us in the lurch! I will give you more for staying with us than the Persian king would ever send you if you deserted us'; and without further delay he sent aboard Adeimantus' ship three talents of silver. So Adeimantus and Eurybiades yielded to bribery and the Euboeans' wishes were gratified; Themistocles, too, made something out of the transaction, for he kept the rest of the money himself. Nobody knew he had it, and the two men who had received their share imagined that it came from Athens especially for the purpose. These were the circumstances which led to the Greeks engaging the Persians on the Euboean coast, and I will now describe the battle itself.

The Persians reached Aphetae early in the afternoon, and saw for themselves what they had previously heard reported – namely that a small Greek force was concentrated at Artemisium. At once they were eager to engage, in the hope of capturing the Greek ships. It did not, however, seem advisable to advance, in the first instance, openly to the attack; for the Greeks, seeing them coming, might try to escape, and then, when darkness overtook them, they would be sure to get clear away. This would not do, as the Persians were determined that not even a fire-signaller (as they put it) must be allowed to escape alive. Laying their plans accordingly, they detached a squadron of 200 ships with orders to sail outside Sciathus, in order to escape enemy observation, and then to turn southward round Euboea and into the Euripus by way of Caphareus and Geraestus; in this way they hoped to catch the Greeks in a trap, one squadron taking them in the rear and blocking their retreat, the rest of the fleet pressing upon them from in front. With this purpose in view the two hundred ships were dispatched, while the main body waited – for they did not intend to attack on that day, or until they knew by signal that the squadron coming up the Euripus had arrived. Meanwhile a review of the main fleet was held at Aphetae, and while it was going on the following event occurred. Serving with the Persian force there was a man named Scyllias, a native of Scione and the most accomplished diver of his day, who after the wreck of the Persian ships at Pelion had saved a great deal of valuable property for his masters – besides getting a good deal for himself. This man had apparently been thinking for some time past of deserting to the Greeks, but no opportunity had occurred until then. I cannot say for certain how it was that he managed to reach the Greeks, and I am amazed if what is said is true; for, according to this, he dived under water at Aphetae and did not come up until he reached

Artemisium – a distance of about ten miles. There are other somewhat tall stories, besides this, told about Scyllias – and also a few true ones; as to the one I have just related, my personal opinion is that he came to Artemisium in a boat. In any case, come he did; and on his arrival he lost no time in giving an account to the Greek commanders of all the circumstances of the disaster to the Persian fleet in the storm, and also told them about the squadron which was on its way round Euboea.

The Greek commanders at once proceeded to discuss the situation which this piece of intelligence produced; and after a long debate it was decided to stay where they were until after midnight, and then put to sea to meet the Persians who were coming up the Euripus. However, as time went on and they met with no opposition, they waited till the evening of the following day and then attacked the main enemy fleet, with the intention of testing Persian seamanship and tactics.

When the officers and men of Xerxes' fleet saw the Greeks moving to the attack with such a small force, they thought they were mad and at once got under way themselves, in confident expectation of making an easy capture; nor, indeed, was the expectation unreasonable, in view of the disparity in numbers – the Greek ships being few, and their own many times as numerous, as well as faster. Thus assured of their superiority, they developed a movement to surround the enemy. Those of the Ionians who had been forced to serve with the Persian fleet in spite of their real sympathy with the Greek cause, were much distressed at the sight of the gradual encirclement of the Greeks, and convinced, in view of their apparent weakness, that not a man amongst them would escape alive; those, on the other hand, who welcomed the situation, entered into competition with each other to be the first to win a reward from Xerxes for the capture of an Athenian ship – for throughout the Persian fleet it was the Athenians who were most talked of.

At the first signal for action the Greek squadron formed into a close circle – bows outward, sterns to the centre; then, at the second signal, with little room to manoeuvre and lying, as they were, bows-on to the enemy, they set to work, and succeeded in capturing thirty Persian ships. Amongst the prisoners was Philaon, the son of Chersis and brother of Gorgus the king of Salamis, and a person of repute in the enemy force. The first Greek to take a prize was the Athenian Lycomedes son of Aeschraeus. He was decorated for valour after the battle.

After this success, when darkness put an end to the fighting, the Greeks returned to Artemisium, and the Persians – who had had a considerable shock – to Aphetae. The only Greek in the Persian force to desert and join his countrymen during the action was Antidorus, the Lemnian; the Athenians afterwards showed their appreciation by giving him a grant of land in Salamis.

After dark – the season was midsummer – there was a very violent rainstorm, which lasted all night, accompanied by much thunder from the direction of Pelion. Dead bodies and bits of wreckage, drifting up to Aphetae, fell athwart the bows of the ships which lay there, and fouled the oar-blades of any that were under way; this, and the noise of the thunderstorm, caused a panic amongst the Persian troops, who began to think their last hour was come: they had, indeed, had much to put up with – for almost before they could draw breath again after the storm at Pelion, which wrecked so many of their ships, they were faced with a hard fight at sea, and now, on top of that, they were exposed to floods of rain, the rushing of swollen streams into the sea, and a tremendous thunderstorm.

For the Persians at Aphetae it was a bad enough night, but it was far worse for the squadron which had been ordered to sail round Euboea, for they were at sea when the storm caught them. Their fate was miserable: just as they were off the Hollows of Euboea the wind and rain began, and every ship, overpowered and forced to run blind before it, piled up on the rocks. God was indeed doing everything possible to reduce the superiority of the Persian fleet and bring it down to the size of the Greek. So much for the disaster off the Hollows.

The Persians at Aphetae were very glad to see the dawn next morning, and did not feel like taking any further risks; it was enough for them, badly shaken as they were, to let the ships lie and attempt nothing for the present. Meanwhile the Greeks received a reinforcement of fifty-three ships from Athens; the arrival of this fresh squadron, together with the news of the loss in the storm of the whole Persian force which was sailing round Euboea, was a great encouragement, and the Greeks, on the strength of it, waiting till the same time as on the previous day, once again put to sea and attacked some

Cilician vessels; these they destroyed and then, at the approach of darkness, they returned to Artemisium.

The Persian commanders were humiliated at receiving such rough treatment from so small a fleet; they were beginning, moreover, to be alarmed at the thought of what Xerxes might do to them; so on the third day they took the initiative, and, without waiting for the Greeks to move, made their preparations and put to sea round about midday. It so happened that these battles at sea took place on the same days as the battles at Thermopylae, and in each case the object was similar – to defend the passage into the heart of Greece: the fleet was fighting for the Euripus just as the army with Leonidas was fighting for the pass. So the Greek cry was to stop the enemy from getting through, while the Persians aimed at destroying the defending forces in order to clear the passage.

Xerxes' fleet now moved forward in good order to the attack, while the Greeks at Artemisium quietly awaited their approach. Then the Persians adopted a crescent formation and came on with the intention of surrounding their enemy, whereupon the Greeks advanced to meet them, and the fight began. In this engagement the two fleets were evenly matched – the Persian, by its mere size, proving its own greatest enemy, as constant confusion was caused by the ships fouling one another. None the less they made a brave fight of it, to avoid the disgrace of defeat by so small an enemy force. The Greek losses both in ships and men were heavy, those of the Persians much heavier. Finally the action was broken off with such results as I have described. On the Persian side it was the Egyptians who came out of it with the best record, their most notable achievement being the capture of five Greek ships together with their crews; of the Greeks the most conspicuous were the Athenians – and in particular Cleinias, the son of Alcibiades, who was serving in his own ship manned by two hundred men, all at his own personal expense.

Both sides were glad when they parted and made all speed back to their moorings. The Greeks, once they were clear of the fighting, did, indeed, manage to possess themselves of the floating bodies and to salve the wreckage; nevertheless they had been so roughly handled – especially the Athenians, half of whose ships were damaged – that they determined to quit their station and withdraw further south. At this point it occurred to Themistocles that if the Ionian and Carian contingents could be detached from the Persian force, the Greeks would be able to deal successfully with the rest; accordingly he called his officers to a conference on the beach, to which the people of Euboea were already driving their herds. Here he told them that he thought he had a plan, which might succeed in depriving Xerxes' fleet of its finest units. For the moment he gave no further details of what the plan was, but merely advised them, in view of the circumstances, to slaughter as many of the Euboean herds as they pleased, as it was better that their own troops should have them than the enemy. He further suggested that every officer should order his men to light fires as usual; as for the withdrawal from Artemisium, he made himself responsible for choosing the proper moment and for seeing that they got home safely. These proposals proved acceptable; so the commanders at once had fires lighted, and the men set to on the herds.

I should add here that the Euboeans had paid no attention to the oracle of Bacis, supposing it to have no significance; they had taken no precautions against the threat of war, either by removing property from the island or by getting in stores, and consequently found themselves in a highly dangerous position. The oracle was as follows:

> When one of foreign speech casts a papyrus yoke upon
>   the sea,
> Bethink you to keep the bleating goats far from Euboea.

This warning they ignored; and the result was great suffering, both then and later, in the troubles which were daily expected.

While the Greeks were thus occupied, their observer arrived from Trachis. The Greeks had employed two, to keep communication between the fleet and the army: at Artemisium Polyas, a native of Anticyra, kept a boat ready to report to the army at Thermopylae any reverse which might be suffered by the fleet, while the Athenian Abronichus, the son of Lysicles, did similar duty with Leonidas, and had a thirty-oared galley always available to report to Artemisium, if the army got into any trouble. It was this Abronichus who now arrived with the news of the fate of Leonidas and his men. The effect was immediate; the Greeks put off their withdrawal not a minute longer, but got under way at once, one after another, the Corinthians leading, the Athenians bringing up the rear.

Themistocles took the fastest ships and called on the way at all the places where drinking water was to be found, and cut notices on the rocks near by for the Ionians to read – as they did when they moved up on the following day. 'Men of Ionia' – his message ran – 'it is wrong that you should make war upon your fathers and help to bring Greeks into subjection. The best thing you can do is to join our side; if this is impossible, you might at least remain neutral, and ask the Carians to do the same. If you are unable to do either, but are held by a compulsion so strong that it puts desertion out of the question, there is still another course open to you: in the next battle, remember that you and we are of the same blood, that our quarrel with Persia arose originally on your account – and fight badly.'

In leaving this message Themistocles probably had two possibilities in mind: in the first place, it might, if the kings did not get to know of it, induce the Ionians to come over to the Greeks, and, secondly, if it were reported to Xerxes and made the ground of an accusation against the Ionians, they would be distrusted and not allowed, in consequence, to take part in engagements at sea.

Immediately after this a native of Histiaea sailed to Aphetae with the news of the Greek withdrawal from Artemisium. The Persians refused to believe it; they put the man under guard and sent off a party of some fast ships to see for themselves. Then, assured that the news was true, they moved at sunrise with the whole fleet to

Artemisium, where they stayed until midday, before going on to Histiaea. They took this town, and overran all the coastal villages of Ellopia, a district belonging to Histiaea. While they were here, a messenger arrived from the king. Before sending him, Xerxes had arranged that of the twenty thousand men in the Persian army who had been killed at Thermopylae, all except about a thousand should be buried in trenches and covered over with earth and leaves, to prevent their being seen by anyone from the fleet. The remaining thousand were left exposed. On reaching Histiaea the messenger had the whole force assembled and delivered his message. 'Fellow-soldiers,' he said, 'the king grants leave for anyone who wants it, to go and see with his own eyes how he fights against the madmen who thought they could beat him.' The announcement was no sooner made than so many people wanted to avail themselves of the king's offer that the supply of boats ran out. All who could, crossed the water and toured the battlefield to see the bodies; some of the corpses were, of course, those of helots, but the sightseers imagined that they were all Spartans and Thespians; however, Xerxes' ludicrous attempt to conceal the number of his own dead deceived nobody. For on one side a thousand corpses lay scattered, and on the other side were the four thousand all lying together in the same spot.

On the day after this, which had been spent in sightseeing, the seamen rejoined their ships at Histiaea and the army with Xerxes set forward on its march. A few Arcadian deserters came in – men who had nothing to live on and wanted employment; they were taken to

Xerxes and questioned about what the Greeks were doing. One Persian conducted the interrogation on behalf of them all, and he was told in reply that the Greeks were celebrating the Olympic festival, where they were watching athletic contests and chariot-races. When he asked what the prize was for which they contended, the Arcadians mentioned the wreath of olive-leaves. This drew from Tritantaechmes, the son of Artabanus, a very sound remark – though it made Xerxes call him a coward; for when he learned that the prize was not money but a wreath, he could not help crying out in front of everybody, 'Good heavens, Mardonius, what kind of men are these that you have brought us to fight against – men who compete with one another for no material reward, but only for honour!'

Meanwhile, immediately after the disaster at Thermopylae, the Thessalians sent a representative to Phocis. They had always been on bad terms with the Phocians, but especially so since the last blow they had received from them. Not many years before the Persian invasion the Thessalians and their allies in full force had invaded Phocis and been defeated with serious losses. The Phocians were blocked up in Parnassus, and their subsequent success was due to a clever piece of work by an Elean named Tellias, who was serving with the Phocians as their diviner; what he did was to pick six hundred good men, cover their bodies and weapons all over with whitewash, and send them on a night attack against the enemy, with instructions to kill everyone they saw who was not whitened like themselves. The Thessalian sentries were the first to see them, and took them for some sort of appalling apparition; then the panic spread to the rest of the troops, who were so badly scared that the Phocians killed four thousand of them, and got possession of their bodies and shields. Half the shields were sent as an offering to the temple at Abae, the other half to Delphi, while from a tenth part of the plunder were made the great statues which stand around the tripod in front of the temple at Delphi, and also the similar figures at Abae.

In addition to breaking out from Parnassus and inflicting this signal defeat on the Thessalian infantry, the Phocians also did irreparable damage to the Thessalian cavalry during an attempted raid. They dug a deep trench across the pass near Hyampolis, put a number of big empty jars in it, and covered them over lightly with soil; then, making the surface smooth and level to conceal the trap, they awaited the attack. The Thessalians galloped up, expecting to sweep all before them, when their horses fell through into the jars and broke their legs. Thus the Thessalians had two reasons for resentment when they sent their representative to Phocis. Their message ran as follows: 'Men of Phocis, now at last you must admit your error, and own that you are not our equals. In the past, while it suited us to be one with the Greeks, we were always considered more important than you; and now our influence with the Persians is so great that a word from us would get you turned out of your country, and sold as slaves into the bargain. All the same, though we have you completely in our power, we are willing to let bygones be bygones: just pay us off with fifty talents, and we undertake to divert the danger which is threatening your country.'

Now the Phocians were the only people in this part of Greece who had not gone over to the Persians, and in my opinion their motive was simply and solely their hatred of Thessaly. If Thessaly had remained loyal, no doubt the Phocians would have deserted to Persia. As it was, when they heard what the Thessalian representative had to say, they refused to pay a penny and declared that they could join Persia just as easily as the Thessalians did, had they been inclined that way; nevertheless they would never willingly prove traitors to Greece. This reply to their message made the Thessalians very angry, and they forthwith offered to act as guides to the Persian army.

From Trachis the army entered the narrow strip of Dorian territory, barely four miles wide, which lies between Malis and Phocis. In old days this region was called Dryopis, and was the mother city of the Peloponnesian Dorians. The Persians did no damage to this part of Doris on their way through; the people in any case were friendly, and the Thessalians wished them to be spared. Passing from Doris into Phocis, they failed to catch the Phocians because they had already cleared out: some of them had gone up into the mountains – the height of Parnassus, called Tithorea, not far from the city of Neon, has plenty of room for a large body of men, and a number of them had climbed up on to it and taken with them all they could move – while the majority had sought shelter with the Locrians of Ozolae and taken their property to Amphissa, the town which stands above the plain of Crisa. All Phocis was overrun; the Thessalians did not let the Persian army miss a bit of it, and everywhere they went there was devastation by fire and sword, and towns and temples were burnt. Along the valley of the Cephisus nothing was spared; Drymus, Charadra, Erochus, Tethronium, Amphicaea, Neon, Pedies, Trites, Elateia, Hyampolis, Parapotamii – all these places were burnt to the ground, including Abae, where there was a temple of Apollo richly furnished with treasure and offerings of all kinds. There was an oracle there, as indeed there is today; the shrine belonging to it was plundered and burnt. A few Phocians were chased and caught near the mountains, and some women were raped successively by so many Persian soldiers that they died.

At Panopes, which they reached by way of Parapotamii, the army divided and one division, the stronger and more numerous, proceeded with Xerxes towards Athens, entering Boeotia at Orchomenus. All the Boeotians had gone over to the enemy, and their towns were protected by Macedonians, sent by Alexander, to make it clear to Xerxes that the people of Boeotia were friendly to him. The other division of the army made with their guides for the temple at Delphi, keeping Parnassus on their right. They, too, devastated all the parts of Phocis through which they passed, and burnt the towns of Panopes, Daulis, and Aeolidae. This division was detached from the main body of the army for the special purpose of plundering the temple at Delphi, and bringing its treasures to Xerxes; I have been told that he was better acquainted, from descriptions continually coming to his notice, with everything of importance there than with his own property at home, and especially with the precious objects which had been presented to the shrine by Croesus, the son of Alyattes.

The news of the approach of the Persians caused consternation at Delphi; and in their terror the people asked the god's advice as to whether they should bury the sacred treasures or get them out of the country. The god replied that they were not to be disturbed, for he was well able to guard his own. This being decided, the Delphians began to think about saving themselves; they sent their women and children across the water into Achaea, and most of the men took to the mountains in the summits of Parnassus, and stored their movable property in the Corycian cave, while a few of them made their escape to Amphissa in Locris. All abandoned the town except sixty men and the Priest of the oracle.

The Persians were now close at hand and within sight of the temple, when suddenly the Priest, whose name was Aceratus, saw weapons lying on the ground in front of the shrine – they were the sacred weapons which no human hand may touch, and they had been brought out from their place within. He hastened to report this portent to the other Delphians who were still in the town. Meanwhile the enemy were drawing quickly nearer, and when they reached the temple of Athene Pronaea even greater portents happened to them than what I have just recorded. It is marvellous enough that weapons of war should move of their own accord and appear upon the ground outside the shrine; but what occurred next is surely one of the most amazing things ever known – for just as the Persians came to the shrine of Athene Pronaea, thunderbolts fell on them from the sky, and two pinnacles of rock, torn from Parnassus, came crashing and rumbling down amongst them, killing a large number, while at the same time there was a battle-cry from inside the shrine. All these things happening together caused a panic amongst the Persian troops. They fled; and the Delphians, seeing them on the run, came down upon them and attacked them with great slaughter. All who escaped with their lives made straight for Boeotia. There is a story, I have learned, amongst those who got away, that there was yet another miraculous occurrence: they saw, so they said, two gigantic hoplites – taller than ever a man was – pursuing them and cutting them down. According to the Delphians, these were Phylacus and Autonous, local heroes who have enclosed plots of ground near the temple, which are held sacred to them – that of Phylacus lies along the road above the temple of Pronaea, and that of Autonous is near the spring of Castalia under the peak called Hyampia.

The rocks which fell from Parnassus were still there in my time; they lay in the enclosure round the shrine of Pronaea, where they embedded themselves after crashing through the Persian troops. So that was how these people took their departure from the Holy Place at Delphi.

The Greek fleet, having sailed from Artemisium, brought up, at the Athenians' request, at Salamis. The Athenians'

object in urging the commanders to take up this position
was to give themselves an opportunity of getting their
women and children out of Attica, and also of discussing
their next move – as their present circumstances, and
the frustration of their hopes, most evidently demanded.
They had expected that the full strength of the Peloponnesian army would concentrate in Boeotia to hold up
the Persian advance, but now they found nothing of the
sort; on the contrary, they learned that the Peloponnesians were concerned only with their own safety and
were fortifying the Isthmus in order to protect the Peloponnese, while the rest of Greece, so far as they cared,
might take its chance. It was this news which led to the
request to the fleet to put in at Salamis.

While, therefore, the rest of the fleet lay at Salamis,
the Athenians returned to their own harbours, and at
once issued a proclamation that every one in the city
and countryside should get his children and all the
members of his household to safety as best he could.
Most of them were sent to Troezen, but some to Aegina
and some to Salamis. The removal of their families was
pressed on with all possible speed, partly because they
wished to heed the warning which had been given them
by the oracle, but more especially for an even stronger
reason. The Athenians say that the Acropolis is guarded
by a great snake, which lives in the temple; indeed they
believed so literally in its existence that they put out
monthly offerings for it to eat in the form of a honey-
cake. Now in the past the honey-cake used always to be
consumed, but on this occasion it was untouched. The
temple Priestess told them of this, and in consequence,

believing that the goddess herself had abandoned the Acropolis, they were all the more ready to evacuate the town. As soon as everything was removed, they rejoined the fleet on its station.

There were some other Greek ships which had been ordered to assemble at Pogon, the harbour of Troezen, and these, when news came through that the fleet from Artemisium had put into Salamis, left Troezen and joined it. Thus the fleet was larger than it had been at the battle of Artemisium, and made up of ships from more towns. It was still under the same commander, Eurybiades, the son of Eurycleides – a Spartan but not of the royal blood; but the city which furnished by far the greatest number of ships, and the fastest, was Athens. The composition of the fleet was as follows: 16 ships from Lacedaemon, the same number from Corinth as at Artemisium, 15 from Sicyon, 10 from Epidaurus, 5 from Troezen, 3 from Hermione. The people of all these places except Hermione are of Dorian and Macedonian blood, and had last emigrated from Erineus, Pindus, and Dryopis. The people of Hermione are Dryopes, and were driven out by Heracles and the Malians from the country now called Doris.

The contingents mentioned above were from the Peloponnese; from outside the Peloponnese there were, first, the Athenians with 180 ships, half the whole fleet. These were manned by Athenians only, for the Plataeans did not serve with them at the battle of Salamis, because during the withdrawal from Artemisium, when the fleet was off Chalcis, they landed in Boeotia on the opposite shore and set about conveying their property and households to a place of safety, and were consequently left behind. When what is now called Greece was occupied by the Pelasgians, the Athenians, a Pelasgian people, were called Cranai. In the reign of Cecrops they acquired the name of Cecropidae. At the succession of Erechtheus they changed their name to Athenians; and when Ion, the son of Xuthus, became general of their armies, they took from him the title of Ionians.

From Megara there was the same number of ships as at Artemisium; then there were 7 from Ambracia, and 3 from Leucas. The Ambraciots and Leucadians are Dorians from Corinth. Of the island states Aegina contributed 30 ships. The Aeginetans had others in commission, but these were employed in guarding their own island; their best thirty were the ones which fought at Salamis. The Aeginetans are Dorians from Epidaurus; the island used to be known as Oenone. Next was the squadron from Chalcis; this consisted of the same twenty ships which served at Artemisium; from Eretria there were the original 7. These two peoples are Ionians. Ceos (the Ceans are Ionians from Athens) sent the same number as before, and Naxos 4. The Naxian contingent, like those from the other islands, had been sent to join the Persians, but disobeyed orders and joined the Greeks at the instigation of Democritus, a man of distinction who was then in command of a trireme. The Naxians are Ionians of Athenian blood. Styra provided the same ships as at Artemisium, and Cythnus one trireme and a penteconter. The Styreans and Cythnians are Dryopes. Seriphus, Siphnus, and Melos also took part – they were the only islands not to make their submission to Persia. All these states are situated on this side of the river

Acheron and the country of the Thesprotians, who are neighbours of the people of Ambracia and Leucas – the two most distant places to contribute to the fleet. Beyond them, there was only one community – Croton – which helped Greece in her hour of danger; the Crotoniats sent one ship, under the command of Phayllus, a man who had won three victories at the Pythian games. The Crotoniats are of Achaean blood. All the contingents consisted of triremes, except the Melian, Siphnian, and Seriphian, which were penteconters. The Melians, who are of Lacedaemonian blood, sent two, the Siphnians and Seriphians, who are Ionians from Athens, one each. The total number of warships (excluding the penteconters) was 378.

When the commanders of the various contingents I have mentioned met at Salamis, a council of war was held, and Eurybiades called for suggestions, from anyone who wished to speak, on the most suitable place for engaging the enemy fleet in the territory still under their control – Attica was excluded, as it had already been given up. The general feeling of the council was in favour of sailing to the Isthmus and fighting in defence of the Peloponnese, on the grounds that if they were beaten at Salamis they would find themselves blocked up in an island, where no help could reach them, whereas if disaster overtook them at the Isthmus, they could find refuge amongst their own people. This was the view of the Peloponnesian officers. While the discussion was still going on, a man arrived from Athens with the news that the Persians had entered Attica and were firing the whole country. This was the work of the division of the army under Xerxes which had taken the route through Boeotia; they had burnt Thespia after the inhabitants had escaped to the Peloponnese, and Plataea too, and then entered Attica, where they were causing wholesale devastation. The Thebans had told them that Thespia and Plataea had refused to submit to Persian domination: hence their destruction. The march of the Persian army from the Hellespont to Attica had taken three months – and the actual crossing of the strait an additional one; it reached Attica during the archonship of Calliades.

The Persians found Athens itself abandoned except for a few people in the temple of Athene Polias – temple stewards and needy folk, who had barricaded the Acropolis against the invaders with planks and timbers. It was partly their poverty which prevented them from seeking shelter in Salamis with the rest, and partly their belief that they had discovered the real meaning of the Priestess' oracle – that 'the wooden wall would not be taken'. The wooden wall, in their minds, was not the ships but the barricade, and that would save them.

The Persians occupied the hill which the Athenians call the Areopagus, opposite the Acropolis, and began the siege. The method they used was to shoot into the barricade arrows with burning tow attached to them. Their wooden wall had betrayed them, but still the Athenians, though in imminent and deadly peril, refused to give in or even to listen to the proposals which the Pisistratidae made to them for a truce. All their ingenuity was employed in the struggle to defend themselves; amongst other things, they rolled boulders down the slope upon the enemy as he tried to approach the gates, and for a long time Xerxes was baffled and unable to take them. But in the end the Persians solved their problem: a way of access to the Acropolis was found – for it was prophesied that all Athenian territory upon the continent of Greece must be overrun by the Persians. There is a place in front of the Acropolis, behind the way up to the gates, where the ascent is so steep that no guard was set, because it was not thought possible that any man would be able to climb it; here, by the shrine of Cecrops' daughter Aglaurus, some soldiers managed to scramble up the precipitous face of the cliff. When the Athenians saw them on the summit, some leapt from the wall to their death, others sought sanctuary in the inner shrine of the temple; but the Persians who had got up first made straight for the gates, flung them open and slaughtered those in sanctuary. Having left not one of them alive, they stripped the temple of its treasures and burnt everything on the Acropolis. Xerxes, now absolute master of Athens, dispatched a rider to Susa with news for Artabanus of his success.